MAKING

COLLEGE

RIGHT

MAKING COLLEGE RIGHT

&Heretical Thoughts
Practical Proposals

W I L L I A M   C A S E M E N T

NATIONAL ASSOCIATION OF SCHOLARS

New York

Printed in the United States of America

ISBN-10: 0615626920
ISBN-13: 9780615626925

National Association of Scholars
8 West 38th Street
New York, New York 10018

CONTENTS

INTRODUCTION i

1. DOES COLLEGE COST TOO MUCH? 1

2. RANKING COLLEGES. 25

3. AFFIRMATIVE ACTION AND ELUSIVE EQUALITY 51

4. LEGACIES, FINANCE, AND FAIRNESS 79

5. BIG-TIME "AMATEUR" SPORTS 99

6. COLLEGE GOES TO HIGH SCHOOL. 127

7. QUADRUPLE WHAMMY ON THE CURRICULUM. 145

8. LIBERAL LEARNING NEEDS A NEW P-R CAMPAIGN . . .177

Notes. 197

Index. 209

INTRODUCTION

American higher education is in a state of disarray, and in some ways downright dysfunction. The system that prepares a large share of our nation's young adults for their occupational and civic roles in the 21st century is unfit to serve us effectively. There are major problems that need to be fixed. To analyze all of the problems is beyond the scope of any one book, but standing out among them as highly visible and especially significant – the ones I tackle – are the cost of attendance that continually rises faster than inflation and puts many students well into debt at graduation, mania over attending prestigious schools, controversial admissions preferences for certain groups of students, the commercialism of big-time sports, the practice of shifting the teaching of basic college courses to high schools, and the ineffectiveness of a general-education curriculum that leaves students bereft of essential knowledge. There are other problems, too, but if cost, admissions, basic learning, and the largest extracurricular distraction can be dealt with successfully, the correction our higher education system needs will be well on its way.

To hear that one of our nation's most respected industries is in trouble may surprise many people. American colleges are staffed by an army of experts with high intellects and Ph.D. training. Our institutions are respected around the globe, and students from other countries come here to get in on the excellence and enjoy the cachet their degrees will carry. With that kind of clout, how can the system be in bad shape? A number of commentators who are familiar with it have voiced their concerns, and the indicators they note are often visible to anyone who is watchful and thoughtful. But as we saw with the recent collapse of our financial institutions and automakers, obvious danger signals can be overlooked, or at least tolerated, when life in general is good. And the situation is clouded when the institutions in question put a positive spin on what common sense should tell us are questionable ideas and practices.

What the forces controlling the system want to deflect attention away from is that the basic function collegiate institutions are meant to perform has become overshadowed by other functions and diverted by wrongheaded thinking. Those forces include not only prominent colleges and other ones that follow their lead, but also a large testing agency, a widely read magazine, and a national athletics organization. The front they put up would have us believe that

- skyrocketing tuition is needed to pay for undergraduate teaching, and not to support research, graduate programs, sports teams, construction of facilities, and public-service projects;
- big-time college sports are merely an elite form of amateur athletics;
- a beauty-contest-like survey, dressed up with irrelevant statistics, can tell us which college is best, next best, best after that, and so on;
- admissions preference for the sons and daughters of alumni is critical for fundraising;
- the academic mismatch created by affirmative-action admissions is acceptable collateral damage in the quest for diversity;

- a curriculum made up of mostly specialized courses, and heavy on diversity themes, somehow morphs into a solid liberal arts foundation for a college degree;
- high school teachers not qualified to teach in college, teaching high school students not qualified to be in college, with a syllabus listing a college textbook – should add up to college credit.

And these are only some of the deceptions that have come to pass as a representation of reality and basis for good policy. They are main themes that paint the picture broadly. For detail, each comes with an apparatus of supporting misinformation.

How did higher education get to be in this condition? Where did the features come from that we're not supposed to notice as distorted? Historically, they've appeared within the last 50 years, although some have antecedents stretching back much further while others are strictly recent phenomena. They came at a time when the U.S. was greatly expanding access to college. During the last half century many schools were enlarged and many new ones were established, not only to accommodate population growth, but to increase the percentage of people going on to the postsecondary level. Acquiring advanced learning became a common thing to do. Academia was in a fired-up growth mode. But besides putting more students in school, there was another aspect to the growth – the mission was changing. The traditional model that had emphasized undergraduate teaching evolved to include much more than that, and teaching itself took on new complexities. The industry's vision of itself was reshaped. It can be argued that in our society's evolution, complicated demands have naturally led institutions in various fields to modernize and diversify, and that we should expect higher education to keep up with the times. But with any field, the key question to ask is whether change has been for the good. Is the newer model a superior one? The answer in this case is that in many ways it's not. While the original product it provides now reaches a mass market, changes in that product have put its quality in jeopardy, and other products have taken on more importance so as to crowd it and reduce the place it occupies.

After this glimpse at the history of the current situation, let me note the direction where I don't want to take the discussion, and the one where I do. I don't look longingly at the past and wish we could turn back the clock. There was no prior golden age of higher learning that devolved into the present and that would make life better if we could escape to it. In the mid 20th century, when the problems I key on were either nonexistent or far less developed than today, the profile of collegiate institutions included much we clearly want to leave behind us – when they served a considerably smaller portion of the population, racial segregation still ruled at many schools, women were routinely channeled into nursing and teaching, McCarthyism was the political correctness, doing research meant going to a card catalog consisting of thousands of index cards in little drawers, and information for college-bound high school students was largely limited to what was printed in college catalogs, for example. The academic world has evolved in many good ways to go along with the problematic ones. The point is to move forward with a healthy appreciation for the former and a healthy skepticism about the latter.

In doing that, something else I want to avoid is getting caught up in a grand metaphysics, a structural scheme that identifies a web of causation and interconnections among various problems. As a philosopher, I find that sort of study fascinating, but it doesn't fit with the present project. The one general principle I begin with is that colleges today have been co-opted by various forces that don't have teaching the basic undergraduate curriculum at heart. Beyond that, rather than laying out a particular pattern that holds things together, I take on problems individually. My format, instead of weaving through chapters built upon previous ones, is to present a series of essays. While sometimes one relates to another, each stands on its own. They can be read in any order. Each presents a snapshot of a key problem that needs to be fixed in order to improve the state of higher education. While all of the problems need fixing, they can be addressed individually and don't have to be taken on comprehensively.

Where my tendency as a philosopher shows through, rather than in the schematizing I want to avoid, is in my method of questioning. My intention is to dig into the rationale that the controllers of academia present to justify the way they operate. To put it succinctly, I interrogate their persona. What's exposed is a collection of mistaken claims and rationalizations that, because they come from leaders in the industry, are generally accepted as true or proper, or at least as reflecting unfortunate but necessary conditions. People close enough to colleges' operations to think critically about them often voice suspicions that what's going on is being misrepresented. Parents of college students, trustees and public officials that colleges answer to, alumni when they're asked to give money to "good old alma mater," and college employees themselves may roll their eyes when they hear a rendition of the party line that glosses over conspicuous oddities. But they usually lack the amount of incisive analysis they might like. I hope to provide it.

The process of debunking involves the use of statistics and other factual information. I'm not shy about citing data – dollar amounts and percentages, legal precedents, lists of items from the curriculum, and so on. But my emphasis is on the practical logic of what the data point to. I build a case on persistent cross-examination that reveals the faulty nature of the received wisdom from the higher education establishment. After that, the emphasis turns toward ideas for reform. Some of my proposals are simple, others complex, and several are unorthodox enough that they might be taken as tongue-in-cheek. (Readers can decide for themselves about that.) What none of them are is timid. Depending on what needs fixing, they run from – abolish it, to regulate it, compete with it, sell it off, or at least give it a major overhaul. When the condition of higher learning today is made clear, it becomes obvious that the correction it requires is considerable. A bold analysis is needed to recognize what's wrong, and an equally bold course of action is needed to make things right.

To speak as strongly as I do against the powers that be amounts to nothing short of heresy in the collegiate world. The subtitle for the book denotes that level of nonconformity. When the manuscript was nearly complete, I submitted three of the essays as a sample to a leading university press. The editor was enthusiastic, and eager to see the full product. Knowing that I was asking the establishment to acknowledge its demons in print, at least through its own sponsorship, I'd held back on showing the pieces that would be considered most offensive. When I did send them in, the verdict came back that I deal with issues that are "quite controversial," in a way that is "*too* heretical," and it's unlikely any university press would publish my project. I pushed too many wrong buttons and pushed too hard. An element of dissidence is acceptable, and in some instances even considered respectably avant-garde. In fact, through its publishing arm, higher education puts out many self-critical books. But they stay within certain bounds. Outside those bounds are thoughts that are forbidden and unforgivable. Writers who promote those thoughts don't publish with university presses.

The point to be taken from my tale of a publisher is that the posturing the academic establishment does to justify the way it operates makes room for criticism. The orthodoxy will absorb it to an extent. Beyond that, there's a refusal to recognize the changes that are needed in how higher education thinks about itself and the ways of action that are the result of that refusal. Analysts with a critical eye can see an industry in trouble through obvious danger signals like exorbitant pricing, questionable product quality, outsourcing to unqualified parties, skimming revenue to support outside projects, and a sales approach that encourages racial discrimination and favoritism for the well-connected. The managers on the inside have heard all of this, and they move ahead on their present course with the seeming assumption that the explanations they give to support it will outweigh critics' protests about what's wrong.   In time, as more people become better informed of the breadth and details of the difficulties, the industry's leadership may feel enough pressure to begin the sweeping changes that are needed. This book is an effort in that direction.

DOES COLLEGE COST TOO MUCH?

The price of going to college increases annually at rates well beyond inflation, while consumers – the students and their parents who pay the bills – find themselves going deeper into debt to cover it. What are they paying for, they ask? Colleges, besides charging more, continually seek out larger donations and grants and government subsidies. But money from those other sources doesn't hold tuition in check. Everything that's taken in, school officials inform us, is needed to function well in good times and limp along when times are tough. Politicians and policy analysts join consumers in wondering why so much money is needed to deliver higher learning. All of this condenses into a simple message that draws reinforcement from the media and reverberates through the general public – College Costs Too Much!

College leaders, for their part, say the issue is more complicated than to be understood in a rally cry. They give several explanations for why the situation isn't as bad as people may think, and for how they're doing the best they can to hold prices at a reasonable level while still offering high-quality learning. In a fair assessment of what colleges charge, we're told, financial aid should be taken into account, along with the advantage having a college degree gives in the job world. Then there's the increasing financial burden institutions face in order to keep up with the times – with our ever more complicated and technologically advanced society. These are all relevant factors, but when they've been considered, the expense college students must meet is still formidable. Is it too high? What can be done about it?

The price tag for a year at college for a full-time undergraduate student can range from less than $10,000 for someone who lives frugally at home and attends a community college to over $50,000 at an elite private school. That's the sticker price – regardless of how much of it is paid by the student and how much by other parties through financial aid grants – for tuition and fees plus room and board, but without books and personal expenses. The huge variation is accounted for mostly by tuition. Moving inward from the extremes to national averages, we find tuition to be about $3,000 at community colleges (excluding California, where it is much cheaper), $7,500 for in-state students at public four-year schools and $20,000 out-of-state, $27,000 at private not-for-profit schools and $14,000 at for-profit schools. Room and board for someone not living at home is figured at $8,000 to $10,000 regardless of the type of institution. The case for college being too costly begins here, but it needs a background to put it into perspective.

In 1980 the average tuition at private colleges was 20 percent of median family income – today it's 50 percent. At public colleges the jump was from 4 percent to 11 percent. By another reckoning, over the last three decades, while inflation was up 100 percent, tuition grew by more than 400 percent and even surpassed the rise in health care by nearly double. Room and board hikes, too, were out of proportion, exceeding general increases in housing and food prices by about 40 percent and 10 percent respectively. And to drive home the point that consumers' wallets are being affected, there are data about student indebtedness. In the mid 1990s fewer than half of the students at four-year schools took out loans, whereas today the figure is two-thirds. The average amount owed at graduation is $25,000, up from $18,500 in 2004, and that's without figuring in credit-card debt or money borrowed by parents.

LOOKING BEHIND THE PRICE

Overall these numbers are daunting, although less so for community colleges. Three thousand dollars plus books and living expenses sounds much better than the prices for schools in the other categories. But for all categories, the amount of debt is pushing up fast. When colleges go on the defensive to explain themselves, their first reaction is usually to point out that most students don't pay full sticker price, but a lesser figure discounted by grants and scholarships. Need factors in, and many schools are proud to say they meet 100 percent of it for all or a large majority of their students, although that pledge can be misleading since much of the amount covered is in the form of loans that don't lower the cost. Still, there is often a significant decrease from the publicly announced price. About a third of all college students pay full fare, with two thirds getting reductions that vary from a small figure to all of it.

What colleges are doing, it's sometimes said as tuition goes up sharply, is use the full price paid by those who can afford it to subsidize those who can't. In fact, some of the tuition money is given back in grants that schools take from their own coffers, separate from government grants, to reduce what needy students pay. The implication carried in this Robin Hood principle is that the effect of rising tuition falls on the wealthy. In economists' terms, tuition functions like a progressive tax, although colleges might prefer to be thought of as showing their social conscience.

If the majority of students don't pay full price, and some are far from it, and the process of setting the price is designed to be an equalizer among economic groups, has the complaint that college is too costly been answered? Unfortunately, no. Progressive intentions aren't being fulfilled. Students of all income levels continue to borrow larger amounts to pay for their higher education. And while the government grants that low-income students get (averaging several thousand dollars) help to lessen their pain, institutional grants go to the wealthiest students nearly as often (30 percent) as to the poorest (40 percent) and for larger amounts (averaging $1,500 more). The reason needy students don't get more institutional grant money is that much of what is given out is in the form of merit scholarships. Often that goes to students with little or no need, nullifying the Robin Hood principle. Debt is the telling factor that sinks the equalization claim. While grants hold the debt back to an extent, to know that a major hurt isn't as bad as it first seems is only mildly comforting when there is still a noticeable pain and it's growing. And even if redistributing the the pain were successful, that would miss the point as well. No one wants to pay too much, whether they're getting subsidies that help or they're well-heeled and don't need them. The financial aid argument merely tells us that a cost people find exorbitant is less exorbitant than it could be.

But is it exorbitant? An alternative way of thinking tells us not to be afraid of it, not to fall in with criticism that sees cost as a burden. While wanting to minimize it is a normal impulse, we should consider the positive effects cost leads to. One view here treats it as an incentive. Many higher education institutions in Europe are free or have only a minimal charge, and as a result students are known to stretch out an enjoyable way of life and stay much longer than needed to complete a degree. In the U.S. we sometimes see students extending their stay at public colleges, but hardly ever at the expensive private ones. When people give up something dear to them in order to acquire learning, they treat it more seriously than when it's easily available. They work at their studies harder and are more inclined to complete their degrees so they can get out into the world and apply their knowledge.

Another view says that while college may be expensive, it's well worth it. The rising cost may still not be catching up with true value. That happens because the item being purchased is something special. Unlike with routine goods and services, acquiring a college education is making an investment for a lifetime. And it can't be lost, can't be taken back. Moreover, the yield on the investment is substantial. While figures vary somewhat by source, they show that bachelor's degree holders (without graduate study) earn 75 percent more than people with only a high school diploma do. Going to college pays off. When people experience sticker shock, and face loans, they should keep the overall gain in mind.

These appeals to see the cost of college in circumspect terms derive from reasonable business principles. But the principles are misdirected, and the result gives us platitudes more than reliable insights into the world of college finance. If we accept that paying for their education is an incentive for students, we're left with the question of how much is enough to ensure their diligence. Has the cost today already gone beyond that point for most of them? Regardless of their European counterparts, if American students extend their time in college, it's more likely because they're stopping out to take a job to pay for their studies, or they've changed majors, or they've been closed out of required courses, than because they're relishing an easy life. And besides incentive for the buyer, what about incentive for the seller – the colleges? Do they have a reason to be concerned about overcharging? How will they determine they've reached that point if cries of pain from buyers fail to do it?

This point about recognizing a threshold applies to the investment argument as well. The long-term benefit from attending college is substantial, but that doesn't mean the cost to achieve it is acceptable. The time period for paying off loans to finance it begins when graduates are just starting out in the work world and have the least earning potential of their careers. The cost for lifetime gain can be overpowering in the short term. And it's out of line with the rest of the economy. Not only is it rising at an inordinate rate, but there's nothing to hold it in check. Other investments are subject to periodic balancing – lowering of prices – due to competition, as with the stock market and the housing market. It hasn't happened with colleges. If that comparison seems questionable – something permanent and intangible to things that are not – then consider health care. The cost there is rising faster than inflation, but not as fast as higher education. Rising prices for college carry the notorious distinction of not only being out of line with other prices, but of being unstoppable.

Portraying cost as an incentive works no better than the financial aid argument does as a response to the ever-increasing price tag for college. At best they deflect the issue rather than facing it head on. Neither tells us why the large increases are necessary. That leaves the third line of explanation colleges rely on. With the progression of time, they're being asked to do more with less – to expand the service they provide while relying less on non-tuition sources as payment. A growing population of high school graduates, and society's demand for better educated workers, mean the number of people going to college is rising. Colleges have expanded to accommodate more students – from roughly 12 million (7 million full-time) in 1980 to 18 million (11 million full-time) today – and, of course, the expansion has required funding. But when more is needed, funding from a key source is failing to keep up. The portion of college budgets that comes from state subsidies has stagnated and in some states has declined, leaving schools struggling to make up for what they used to count on. To add to the difficulty, the structure of colleges has become more complex, and public expectations of what should be available are more demanding than ever before. New fields and subfields of study make for more departments and programs, requiring more faculty specialists along with administrators and staff. And to keep schools functioning in an up-to-date way, new support services have been added. Elaborate computer networks and information technology are part of the modern landscape, along with disability services, multicultural social programming, Title IX compliance, mental health counseling, legal services to deal with sexual malfeasance and wrongful termination claims, risk management teams, and so on. The list of functions that have budget lines might astound even those who work on college campuses, but they're needed to ensure a proper environment for students. As life becomes more complicated, what it takes to provide a college education does too.

This is the picture of well-intentioned, underfunded circumstances colleges would have us believe. If only it were justified. While there are more students to teach, it shouldn't be forgotten that their rising number means added income from their tuition. Are they really a financial burden, or just paying their way? Are they more expensive to educate per student because there are so many of them? Or perhaps less expensive? Basic economic theory says that as production increases, cost per unit produced typically goes down. At least that's so if we assume reasonable efficiency.

Rising enrollment is only part of the picture, of course. Another part – the declining budget share from state funds – is questionable too. For one thing, it applies mainly to public colleges and not to private ones, although the majority of students attend public schools. And it applies to some states more than others, depending on their legislatures' spending priorities. But in all cases where it's claimed, the key question to be asked is whether the budget has actually suffered so that tuition hikes are needed to fill the void. When state funding is compromised, fundraising from private sources often moves in as a replacement. Colleges have pushed hard to increase alumni giving, and to court major donors who pay to have their names attached to buildings, endowed chairs, programs, and scholarships. They draw corporate support in exchange for providing programs business communities want, and get grants from foundations and from the federal government. Dunning and deal making form one of the fastest growing functions found within the structural evolution of higher education today. Offices titled "alumni," "development" (or "advancement"), and "sponsored programs" employ many people and compose a main segment of the complexity colleges have grown into. At a large institution the number of professionals in one of these offices alone can reach forty or fifty.

Colleges might respond by saying they have no choice but to seek funding from these sources. Their operating capital has to come from somewhere. This point is fair, but at the same time it can be misleading. The fact that the budget share from public funds is less and from private funds is more isn't necessarily a cause for alarm or for sympathy. An increase in private money may more than make up for a stingy appropriation from the state. But even if the appropriation isn't stingy – maybe it's quite generous – the portion of the budget coming from public funds will go down if fundraising efforts surpass it. The financial picture can be strong, but appear to be victimized when presented in the language of budget-share percentages. This point won't be lost on legislators who appropriate public funds. Should they be faulted for failing to keep up increases to match the private money colleges raise? When spending the public's money, it makes sense to avoid putting it where there are other sources to make up for it, and to put it instead into places that lack higher education's fundraising capability.

If claims about growing enrollment and loss of state funding are questionable justifications for tuition surges, the answer could still lie in the expanded service colleges offer. If the education students get has improved, this is a reason why it should cost more. Certainly colleges have become more complex, as the argument says. What does that complexity mean? What it doesn't mean is a greater emphasis on teaching. Over the last three decades (1976-2005), when the expansion into what we have today took place, the number of full-time faculty rose 17 percent and the number of part-timers was up 200 percent. During the same period, full-time administrators rose 100 percent and non-faculty professionals nearly 300 percent. Faculty growth was greatly eclipsed by other personnel. The increase in faculty that did occur was mostly in low-wage earners who work for a flat fee per course, typically don't get benefits, and take up little office space. What's more, the better paid category – full-timers – barely held their own with inflation, beating it by less than one percent from 1976-2003. So their salaries weren't absorbing the tuition increases students have faced.

With those increases mostly not going toward teaching, can they still be justified as contributing to learning in other ways? The claim about colleges becoming necessarily complex includes the need for support services that are unique to present times, and that have been added to what college was traditionally when it was less expensive. But unique to present times doesn't mean unique to higher education. Features like computer networks, counseling services, and legal services are important in other industries too. Utilities, manufacturers, hospitals, and so on have developed complex workings, but the cost increase they pass on to the public is far less than we find in the price of college. What's different about college, what accounts for the large army of non-teaching personnel that has been added to it, is its diversity of purpose. The original and philosophical core mission – undergraduate instruction – has been subsumed by other functions that, while they're not new, have grown in importance.

Those other functions are on view especially at large universities, but they're present on a lesser scale at other schools as well. Research – the creation of knowledge and presentation of it to the world beyond students and classrooms – is considered the highest level of intellectual endeavor. Colleges expect it and faculty strive to oblige. Some of the research goes to solving practical problems and improving society and the world in general. Much of it is simply added to the accumulation of knowledge, where the only benefit it serves is to lengthen the researchers' resumes. Several decades ago there was less emphasis on research and more on teaching. In 1970 the average teaching load for regular faculty at the most research-intensive schools was three courses per semester, while today it's one or two. The regular load elsewhere (four-year institutions) was four courses, and occasionally more Today in many places that's been reduced to three and sometimes less, including virtually all of the 100 top-ranked (and typically most expensive) liberal arts colleges.

The next step down in intellectual importance from research is graduate education. The growth that's taken place is an additional force that pulls colleges' emphasis away from teaching undergraduates. Giving advanced degrees, and attaching professional schools like medicine, law, and business to undergraduate colleges began in the late 19th and early 20th centuries. Over time, more and more colleges did this, and today even many small schools run master's degree programs in various fields. Mid-sized schools have pushed master's study to the doctoral level as they've become less than research institutions but more than was envisioned for them until recent times.

Public service is another expanded function. Many schools have organized it into impressive institutes or centers. Programs like summer camps, academic outreach to K-12 schools, adult literacy, social entrepreneurship, homeless advocacy, natural resource conservation, science fairs, soup kitchens, and various others are designed to use higher education's expertise to help in local communities and sometimes on a larger scale. The people power often comes from volunteers – students as well as faculty – but there's an outlay of resources for building space, supplies and basic operating expenses, publicity, administrators' salaries, transportation, and so on. The public service efforts colleges engage in lie at the intersection of intellectual pursuits and life beyond, in part giving knowledge to noncollege learners, and in part putting people and ideas out into communities to deal hands-on with social problems.

Outside of the intellectual sphere entirely, American higher education is in the sports entertainment business. And it caters to our nation's population at-large. Division I teams that act like professional operations play to local crowds that number in the tens of thousands for football and basketball, and in the millions on TV. What's new in recent decades is an increase in the amount of travel for many of the teams as leagues have expanded, as well as longer playing schedules, year-round commitments from athletes, coaches with multimillion dollar contracts and assistant coaches who make more than top professors, and the construction of more elaborate and costly stadiums and arenas. Most of the schools involved lose money at it, but they're committed to the enterprise of spectator sports.

Colleges are also in the lifestyle business – to create an over-all atmosphere of maximum livability for their students. Today's residential campuses feature many new buildings, some of them for academic purposes, but a large share are devoted to what students do with their free time. The trend has been to replace gymnasiums with athletic centers, student unions with multiplex student centers, dormitories with apartments, cafeterias with food courts. The point is to provide all of the creature comforts young adults could want, and to make them available within the confines of the campus. Entertainment is a major feature, with buildings housing pool halls, game rooms,and TV rooms. Planned events, besides sports, include movies, concerts, notable speakers and stage performers, and excursions to local places of interest. And beyond entertainment there are banking services and computer and phone sales and services. Every college has a bookstore that carries the school's line of monogrammed clothing, and perhaps grocery essentials. Most of the students attending college will never in their lives again live in such a self-contained, planned community. School officials say this environment is needed to attract them to attend, and institutions throughout the country scramble to keep up in what they themselves call an "arms race" to create more and better facilities and services. Guides for admissions tours emphasize their schools' fancy extras. Recent fads that carry bragging rights include a climbing wall that simulates a rocky escarpment, and pick-up/drop-off laundry service.

Why has American higher education put so much emphasis on expanding up and out from its primary purpose? No one decreed it should be this way, but it's come to be accepted as the model, with some schools striving for parts of it and other schools for the whole thing. It could be argued that growth is to be expected in successful organizations. But this answer won't satisfy critics who say undergraduate instruction is losing ground in the larger enterprise, and that money collected for it is being used to bankroll other functions. Colleges may say they don't mix monies for their various functions, but this answer isn't satisfying either. The workings of their budgets are confusingly intertwined. Costs to run athletics programs (special tutoring, room and board, elaborate training rooms) may be listed in spending categories outside of athletics. Nonacademic programs may be run out of academic buildings. Extra faculty are hired to teach courses not being taught by regular faculty who spend their time doing research and teaching graduate students. On the other hand, even if the functions are kept separate, the core mission of the college may still lose out. Who's to say how much emphasis should be put on teaching undergraduates? The trend is moving away from it.

The force that holds the model in place is that the colleges with the highest reputations follow it. Other schools strive to be like them to whatever degree they're able. Prestigious universities perform all of the functions. Top-rated small colleges generally go without big-time sports and only some have graduate programs, but they still value research and have teaching loads of two or three courses a semester, emphasize a commitment to public service, and especially, compete to outdo each other with posh buildings and social amenities. The assumption we're left with is that academic excellence is part and parcel of the model. The most highly rated schools, the ones top students flock to apply to, and by doing that help to validate the ratings, are exemplars of the model. Schools that do less beyond the function of instruction, and charge less for that, lag far behind in reputation.

To sum up so far, the answer to the question of whether college costs too much is *Yes*. The telling factor is that tuition is rising far faster than inflation and faster than prices in other industries. The rapid increase, along with the fact that financial aid is often given to students without regard for need, means that students are piling up more and more debt. When we ask why college prices are more than in the past relative to the economy, we find mission creep that involves expenditures well beyond the function of undergraduate instruction. Although colleges are very competitive among themselves to attract students, the market force of competition hasn't held the price of attendance in check. Many consumers still strive to pay for the expanded and expensive institutional model used by prestigious schools. What can be done to counter the trend?

What to Do?

Conventional thinking looks for ways to increase financial aid for students – the kind they don't have to pay back. That means giving larger grants based on need, so loans can be smaller. The federal government is one main source of grants, and they aim their help at the lowest economic echelon. Pleas are often heard to bring these grants into line with rising tuition, but they've lagged far behind. And they provide little relief for the middle class, who are finding it increasingly hard to pay for college. The federal funding is well intentioned and helps to an extent, but it's not nearly enough to deal effectively with the cost level college has risen to. State grants provide help too, but face the same problem of being overwhelmed by cost increases.

The other main source of grant money is colleges themselves. They've awarded larger amounts from their own funds as tuition has risen, but here again it's not what would be needed to keep pace. Much of what they give out is based on merit rather than need, prompting dissenters to point out that if the money was redirected to need-based aid, the amount students require in loans could be reduced. That idea carries a sense of fairness, and it would give truth to the dubious claim colleges make that financial aid works as a cost equalizer against high tuition. There's little prospect, though, that this will happen. Merit scholarships are an important tactic in the competition among schools to recruit strong students. They're afraid to give it up unilaterally (although a few have done that), and joining together en masse would mean they would have to trust each other's actions, as well as face the possibility of a legal challenge for antitrust violation.

As an exception, it should be pointed out that in the past several years a few colleges – private ones with impressively high endowments – have committed to replacing loans with grants for families in the low and sometimes even middle income ranges.

They haven't sworn off merit aid, but can afford to use money of their own to meet all or nearly all need that isn't covered by government grants. These schools are among the ones that charge the highest tuition rates, and their names carry the greatest prestige. Their leadership can influence the thinking of other schools. Unfortunately, the others – the vast majority – can't follow the lead. They have limited funds, and are far from being able to offer a free education to everyone they enroll who has need. The largesse a few can afford isn't an answer that can be applied on a broad scale.

The conventional approach of using financial aid to balance against rising prices doesn't work. The rise is fast, and the aid available is too little. The problem is that the burden of fiscal responsibility falls on the aid rather than on the price. Instead of trying to help students keep up, colleges could slow down. Here is the unconventional approach – figure out how to contain cost rather than how to rise to cover it. Again some people look to the federal government for an answer. And Congress responded in 2008 by instituting cost reporting requirements for colleges and a plan for publicizing the data that are collected. The hope is to shame schools into controlling what they charge, and to make consumers better informed to do comparison shopping. But if colleges and consumers haven't been motivated to change their behavior after all of the publicity in recent years about the high cost of college – cost is still going up and students are still striving to get into the most expensive schools – it's difficult to think that providing more details about the obvious will move them. A stronger measure would be to establish limits on what colleges are allowed to charge. Other industries have been subject to mandated price controls, proponents say, and higher education could be too. This idea faces stiff opposition from the powerful lobby colleges maintain coupled with a long tradition in Washington of leaving colleges more free to operate than other industries in the economy. Higher education falls largely in the nonprofit sector where excesses are more easily excused than the large profits corporations can show. And it commands respect as a bastion of intelligence as well as for its vocal display of concern about social justice. All of this spells a distaste at the federal level for dictating the tuition colleges charge.

Another angle sees a way to capitalize on colleges' nonprofit status to create an indirect push back against tuition. Nonprofit foundations are required to spend 5 percent annually from their endowments to further the purpose for which they were established. If colleges were held to that requirement, the money could be applied to reduce the amount students are charged. The basic thrust of this idea may appeal to many people, but the devil is in the details. Colleges already spend from their endowments. It's a longtime practice, and for the last decade the national average has been between 4 percent and 5 percent annually. So they're not opposed in principle to tapping their holdings. To require all of them to meet the 5 percent figure could help to defray students' costs some, but that percentage may not be a high enough minimum. And many of the schools that would be affected don't have large endowments, so the result of taking a bit more from them would probably yield much less than proponents of this measure are hoping for.

Beyond the question of how much a college spends from its endowment is what the money is used for. Simply requiring a certain payout wouldn't mean it was applied to help students financially. Usually some of it is, and it goes toward the conventional approach of increasing aid through grants rather than holding the standard price of tuition in check. Some of the rest may be spent on instruction, but often it supports the various other functions – research, student lifestyle, and so on – that make up the fulsome form higher education embodies.

It's possible the 5 percent rule could direct the payout toward improving students' finances. But since roughly 60 schools hold two-thirds of all endowment assets, the big money would go toward helping only the tiny portion of the college population that attends them. And those are the schools that already are covering much or all of student need through grants. To spread their holdings further would require the nonprofit equivalent of a windfall profits tax on wealthy institutions, with the money from it being paid out to the rest of the schools. This notion is likely to be no more popular than price controls – legislators would have to put aside the preferential treatment they give to higher education, and then stand up for a radical system of redistributing wealth.

A variety of reasons makes federal mandates for controlling tuition either improbable or unlikely to meet the potential proponents may see in them. But suppose colleges were coaxed or prodded to put on the brakes against runaway price increases. Suppose they were to freeze tuition and hold it that way for several years. The problem for students is far from solved. The price level they're facing after many years when schools were moving too fast still puts them in financial jeopardy. Even a freeze doesn't make prices affordable. The way to do that is by rolling back to a point where they were before consumers of higher learning were amassing mountains of debt – a point where people going to college would still bear a reasonable responsibility for financing their studies, but where that isn't out of line with the cost of other important purchases in their lives.

Price rollbacks are a common part of our economic system, but they're foreign to colleges. The thought of cutting tuition is heretical to followers of the dominant institutional model that costs so much. What's required is to alter the model – to take a hard look at what creates high cost, and figure out what could be reduced or removed. Instead of accepting the complicated and expanded version of what higher education institutions have become, the new plan asks how the basic agenda of teaching the curriculum to undergraduates can be accomplished from a simpler framework that charges students less.

One alteration that's now underway is to substitute online instruction for classroom study. If colleges can offer virtual courses at a lesser expense to themselves, they can pass the savings on to their students. Optimists hail the technology of the Internet as holding the key to cost reduction. But there are two reasons to be cautious. One is that it hasn't been established that virtual courses truly are cheaper. Perhaps it seems intuitive that they should be, but whether they are and how much so may depend on variations in their format. Merely putting up a list of assignments and lecture notes along with a final exam and the professor's email address weighs in on the budget conscious side, but regularly scheduled group meetings in cyberspace, along with frequent individual contacts with the professor and frequent evaluations, may limit class size to the seminar level and use expensive face-to-face technology. As things stand today, some schools offer online courses for lower tuition than their classroom counterparts, but at other schools online is the same price (or nearly so) and in some cases it's more. So far in the virtual revolution, the price for students seems to mirror an institution's existing tuition structure more than to change it.

If colleges are saving money by teaching via the net, it isn't visible in the prices most are charging. Will that change in the future? The prospect looks unlikely given higher education's present trend. Virtual learning is growing, with some large public institutions now encouraging or requiring students to take a designated amount of their coursework online. The schools say they're economizing through that maneuver by converting large lecture courses into an even larger enrollment configuration that doesn't use classroom space. But the savings aren't being passed on to students through tuition relief. Instead, they're absorbed into the overall budget, and tuition continues to go up.

The second caution about online learning is that many people think of it as inferior to the time-honored bricks-and-mortar approach. In particular, the purveyors of higher education themselves are less than convinced of its worth. Various studies have been done, and more will be, to measure the effectiveness of virtual instruction, but it will take a considerable body of favorable evidence to convince skeptical faculty on campuses today, and to answer questions believers have about whether it's good for all students or only for some, for all subjects and courses or only some, and to substitute for all methodologies or just the lecture method. According to a 2009 national survey, substantially fewer than half of the faculty (and especially those at private colleges where the highest prices and often the highest prestige are found) accept "the value and legitimacy of online instruction."

Compounding the problem of virtual schooling's reputation is that it's often associated with for-profit institutions that lie at the bottom of the prestige ladder in higher education. They're not mentioned in the same breath as the elite private schools that have been the last to join the virtual bandwagon. At most of the top brand names, online offerings are limited, although some traditional courses are becoming hybrids by adopting elements of the virtual approach, and a few schools (MIT, Stanford, Carnegie Mellon, Yale) have joined the "open education movement" that puts course materials on the net to be used for free. The MITx program, launched in 2012, goes further by including testing and certificates for course completion for a small fee, thus offering an alternative credentialing model. This model threatens to undercut the pricing structure of on-campus learning at elite colleges. They stand to lose income if they allow students to use MITx for transfer credit. And if they develop their own programs to compete with it, they'll be hard pressed to charge more than their high-profile peer does.

MIT's bold action adds the prestige factor to online learning – a certificate from the school showing mastery of its coursework will garner instant respect. But it leaves unresolved questions about the sort of knowledge students have acquired. Does self-study plus a test equal what happens in a traditional on-campus course? Even the "best" colleges haven't answered that question in a way that generates enthusiasm among their faculty. As long as those schools are hesitant about including online learning in their degree programs (while they make a cheap, bare-bones version of it available for non-degree outsiders), and applicants continue to flock there with a willingness to pay high prices, the potential for virtual learning to bring tuition relief will be limited. The schools that are considered to be the industry's leaders set the pace. If their tuition continues to climb, other schools will follow in their wake as a calculated distance – staying behind the leaders but on an upward trend.

The prestige factor shows through against online instruction just as it does with learning delivered traditionally at schools that defy the dominant institutional model – the ones that offer a college degree for a cheaper price in leaner campus surroundings. Something needs to be done to dispel the notion that the dominant model is best. An image breaker is essential. It could come through the establishment of a new college – one with a no-frills structure and at less expense, yet that's widely recognized to provide the highest quality bachelor's degree. A college of that sort would challenge the mindset that identifies excellence with complexity and cost. The key to the new school, what would make it different from existing ones that are simpler and less expensive than the elites, isn't talented teachers or a solid curriculum, which they may already have. Two of the three main elements that make up a top academic program can be found at unheralded schools. The difference is the level of the students. The new school would take in only top students, and wouldn't operate otherwise. If it were opened with great fanfare, and continued to get publicity as an experiment, it would be a gauge for people to use in evaluating cost.

Is an academically elite but less expensive college a possibility? Could it get top students? Accreditation? Money to start up and operate? If the school pitched itself to cost-conscious high achievers as a place for them to band together, it could expect an abundance of applicants. To draw them to actually attend, the college could put the qualified ones in touch with each other and encourage them to organize and develop friendships so they would feel the support of joining together as educational pioneers. A bold maneuver would be to offer generous financial compensation to committed students if the institution failed to open. The issue of accreditation might be dealt with by setting up the new school as a branch of an existing one that is already accredited.

Financing would be the key to the whole affair. With the number of sources today giving large sums to higher education, and the widely talked about problem of college costing too much, it's reasonable to hope for backing for the project. Just what form the school would take on is variable – public or private, urban/ suburban/rural, residential or nonresidential, perhaps some of the learning done online. But whatever the form, all financial affairs would be fully transparent. They would be on display to show how much or little a frugally run but academically excellent college needs to cost. Consumers would know what they're paying for, and that they shouldn't have to pay more. Brand- name schools would be put on notice that someone else is just as good at a cheaper price, and they should rethink the expensive way they function.

Besides facing them off against a new competitor, it may be possible to give leading colleges a more appealing incentive to change their model and reduce prices. A substantial grant/loan could be made available to a few that would use it to offset the lower tuition they would agree to charge while trimming their institutional structure so the tuition could remain that way in the future. The money a school received would be treated as a grant if it kept to its new plan over a specified period of years, and if not it would become a loan. A large donor matched with a top-ranked college that would reduce tuition significantly would make an interesting experiment worthy of public attention. It would likely bring more applicants to the school, which in turn could push its ranking up a bit. A positive public reaction to the combination of lower prices plus prestige would put pressure on peer institutions to rethink their model. Perhaps none of the top-ranked schools would want to try this plan, feeling confident to rest on their laurels. On the other hand, one in financial straits, or struggling to keep up in admissions with its competitors, or fearful that the tuition bubble may soon burst for expensive colleges, might welcome the opportunity.

All of the preceding ideas for making college more affordable – either for giving money to students or for trying to get schools to rein in their prices – involve actions by people other than the consumers who buy higher education's service. Without relying on those other parties, what can consumers do on their own behalf? Some students have economized on the cost of a bachelor's degree by taking their first two years at a community college and transferring for the last two. This is typically a route for students who didn't shine academically in high school, but it can work for strong students as well although very few choose it. Several factors hold them back that could be answered by one key initiative – self-organization into groups. If a block of a hundred or two hundred top students got together to attend the same community college, they would have the comfort of being among people like themselves. They could feel the camaraderie they'd expect to find only at a highly selective 4-year school. They could join the college's honors program, or get one established, to assure they'd take rigorous courses. Their collective power could be used to find common housing, and for extracurricular programming. The cachet of their group identity could at least partly offset the stigma about going to a community college they would feel from their peers at name-brand schools. And they could still have the edge they might want on their resumes for the future by finishing at a name brand, but at a much cheaper total cost than the cost for students who started there.

Could high school students pull off the kind of organizational feat that's called for? With their social networking habits, and a few parents who would help, they're more than capable. And they could carry their collective power into the transfer process later to a four-year college. If they went on to a public flagship in their home state, they probably wouldn't need it for admission, since many of those schools already take in large numbers from the state's community colleges. And the savings on tuition wouldn't be as great as if they went out of state or to a private school. But especially at private colleges, there are intriguing possibilities. A block of talented students applying to enter at the third-year level could be attractive even to a prominent school with a history of taking only a few transfers. The admissions "yield" would be 100 percent, or almost. That's the gold standard that can't be had otherwise except through "early-decision" commitments. By boosting the number of transfers over its usual number, a school could reduce its freshman enrollment, resulting in greater selectivity and possibly a rise in the rankings. It's likely the transfers would bring some of the economic and ethnic diversity private schools long to have more of. And in terms of finances, the college would gain a cohort of high achievers, whose cost consciousness meant they wouldn't have enrolled as freshman, and need to give them aid for only two years.

Capability and possibility, of course, don't add up to reality. The idea of top students going to a community college as an organized group will seem desperate and far-fetched to many people. Likewise with getting an elite college to transform into a leaner and cheaper model, and with establishing a new elite college on that model. But these proposals are in response to a unique economic situation. The price of a vital product, undergraduate instruction, is ever-increasing, and has been resistant to market principles and to regulation by the federal government. Bewildered consumers are led to believe that in order to have the quality the original product was known for, they must pay for the newer, expanded version that's part and parcel of an expanded product line. With conditions like that, extraordinary measures are needed. If it can be demonstrated that the original and cheaper product can be as good as the expanded version, consumers wanting high quality will feel confident about buying it, name brands will feel competition they're unaccustomed to, and all brands will be pushed to examine how they operate and what they charge for it. Market principles can be awakened – with shock treatment.

2

RANKING COLLEGES

The American public is attuned to product assessment. We're accustomed to reading capsule descriptions done in *Consumer Reports* fashion, and we're enamored with lists that tell us exactly what's best, next best, best after that, and so on. We consult rankings for products in many industries, and they're especially popular for higher education. More people than ever before are applying to more colleges, and they want a way to sort through the mountains of information put out through brochures and websites and the many guidebooks that crowd the shelves in bookstores. What the rankings are designed to tell us in summary form is where to find quality, but along with that comes another factor many people are eager for – prestige. It's not just a strong academic preparation that's in demand, but recognition for the place it comes from. There is a widespread belief that attending a preeminent college is a ticket to a successful career – that it will be a boost for getting into graduate school or for finding a good job. It will get you in the door, and even later carry you further by virtue of the aura surrounding a name or the reach of an alumni network. In other words, status matters!

But does it really? And if so, how much? Students and parents who are looking for a place to get a good education can be misled by popular opinion and salesmanship. The psychology of branding has a strong allure that hides a casualness about substance and common sense. A careful consideration of the situation will show that what the college rankings measure to determine quality is confused and misleading, and the status attached to a school's name is often overrated. The problem isn't that looking for quality is wrong, but that it's easy to look in the wrong places.

U.S. NEWS

Of the many ranking systems that have emerged to answer the public's interest in comparing colleges, one captures an unmatched market share. Standing tall above its competitors and muscling its way through the informatics is *U.S. News and World Report*. Its annual editions of *America's Best Colleges* are consistent number-one best sellers, and they hold a commanding influence over what people think about one college versus another. Other sources rate schools on factors such as selectivity, students' academic satisfaction, financial aid, social life and partying, fire safety, and more. *U.S. News* steers clear of the social scene and focuses on academic worth, boldly listing in rank order each of the best 100-plus national universities, and likewise for national liberal arts colleges, along with 50 to100 master's level schools for each of four geographical regions, and a lesser number of baccalaureate colleges (smaller four-year schools) by region. The detailed inventory includes data in seven categories, some with subcategories, all rolled into a single number that determines rank. The amount of information included is considerable, and the scientific and statistical appearance of the overall product is impressive.

It wasn't always this way. The rankings began in 1983 merely as a poll of college presidents, published in one of the magazine's regular issues, that named the top 25 each of national universities

and liberal arts colleges and top 10 in other brackets. With successful sales, and repeat performances in 1985 and 1987, the rankings then became an annual affair and a stand-alone publication,
and the number of schools ranked gradually increased. Provosts
and admissions deans were added to the poll, and objective material was incorporated to give the assessment more gravitas. Over
time, more objective measures have been included, some dropped,
and their weighting redistributed, with the evolution still ongo-
ing. There is constant tinkering that observers say allows for just
enough change in the ranks to keep the public buying the new
issue each year. The magazine's position is that the changes are
refinements in a constant effort to become better.

Colleges' responses to the rankings have ranged from self-
affirmation to anger to helplessness. While schools getting favorable reviews are quick to publicize them, privately many disdain
the system by which they're produced. The less successful ones are
more apt to be openly reproachful, but organized protest has been
slow in coming, although the Annapolis Group of over a hundred
leading liberal arts colleges has taken a critical stance, and a small
subset has called for a boycott of the peer assessment poll. A more
united effort has been to support an alternative approach to rankings that provides free information about colleges but is nonjudg-
mental. Two major higher education associations sponsor websites of this sort – one for private schools (University and College
Accountability Network) and the other for public schools (College
Portrait). The U.S. Department of Education has its own College
Navigator for both public and private, and the College Board offers
College Search. But as much as these sites can be helpful, *U.S. News*
offers the same sort of information they do through its online version – plus its popular list of best to worst schools that so many
people are anxious to see – for a modest fee.

Overall, colleges know that *U.S. News* is a difficult force to
oppose, and short of a strong common front against it, including

institutions of all types and featuring the big names the magazine counts on for cachet, their capabilities are limited. The magazine, too, knows its dominant position and professes to be unafraid of resistance. It has declared that if the regular participants in the poll refuse to cooperate, replacements can be found. And it knows that colleges can't deny access to the objective data it uses in its ranking formula, since that information is available on college websites and through other sources.

Finding fault with the *U.S. News* rankings isn't difficult. There is plenty to dislike. One main concern is that the players in the game – the rankers as well as the ranked – are not playing fairly. It's obvious to anyone familiar with higher education that the taxonomy features brand names. In the two most prestigious categories – national universities and liberal arts colleges – well-known schools get top billing and lesser known ones do not. Is this a natural reflection of the quality of the schools, or is another influence involved? When in the late 1980s the rankings first took on a serious tone by adding objective data to the peer assessment, a set of categories along with weighting for them was needed to create a formula. As the story goes from a journalist who interviewed an insider at the magazine, when the initial formula was ready and was tested, and it put an unheralded school at the top of the list, the designers then went back to the drawing board and made adjustments that had Ivy League schools take the lead. The magazine began with its notion of who is best and presented data that confirmed that notion. All polls since then have carried the legacy of that notion, and while many adjustments have been made in the formula, and there has been some upward and downward mobility among the colleges, the pecking order has remained relatively stable. When it happens that a new wrinkle in the formula threatens stability, it's duly smoothed out, as when one national university vaulted from No. 9 to No.1 in a single year, surpassing the more storied reigning elite. While such an occurrence might have been squelched internally and not have shown up in print, this one stayed. However, another adjustment was made the next year, moving that school downward.

What can be said in defense of the way the magazine created and has maintained its ranking system? That it acted in a reasonable way to ensure that the brand names already known for quality are used as models and get proper treatment? But that begs the question of what constitutes quality, and throws open just what categories should be included in a formula to measure it, not to mention the weighting each should get. A harsh pronouncement says the books were cooked from the start. A philosophical reaction recognizes the arbitrary nature of the enterprise, and calls for a thorough review and debunking of a pseudoscience that for two decades has passed for expertise on higher education.

While the controllers of the *U.S. News* ranking system have played fast and loose with it, some of the colleges it ranks have done so as well. College officials have carefully scrutinized the formula that's used and have figured out ways to gain an edge in the data they submit for some of its categories. While instances of outright fraud are not unheard of, usually the practices lie in the shadowy realm of rationalized deceit. A trick for improving on average SAT (or ACT) scores is to leave out remedial students, international students, and students admitted any time during the year other than the fall. One school has gone so far as to offer a financial bonus to freshmen who retake their standardized test for a higher score. Some schools have adopted a "test optional" policy, allowing applicants to not send in test scores but treating them equally with ones who do. The reason for dropping the testing requirement may be above board, but the effect inflates the score range a school reports by leaving out low scores from students who were admitted without submitting them.

Acceptance rate can be lowered in several ways – by counting anyone as an applicant who begins the application process but doesn't finish it, counting as rejects students who were turned down for specific programs but accepted into other programs, and being stingy on acceptances while admitting many students from a waiting list but counting them as rejects. Loosely defined, "applications" can be increased by providing a simple one page preliminary form that is submitted online for free. The alumni giving rate can be increased by soliciting a large gift from a single donor who gives in the names of numerous alumni, and maintained by spreading a donation over several years.

When colleges engage in sketchy reporting, they may fall into the self-justification that the system they're forced to report to is measuring irrelevancies. This notion, of course, disregards fairness to the many schools that act honestly, but the point about what the *U.S. News* formula measures is well taken. Some parts of the formula are indeed irrelevant, and others are laden with mistaken assumptions. The most heavily weighted category (a quarter of the total score) is peer assessment – the poll in which presidents and admissions deans rate other institutions of a similar type (national university, master's level, etc). Fewer than half of those polled actually respond, but what do any of them know about what goes on at other schools? Their job is to be experts on what happens at their own schools, not to have a comprehensive knowledge of what happens elsewhere, which would be more than a full time job in itself. The poll ends up being what many characterize as a beauty contest – based on superficiality, much of which may be influenced by reading the *U.S. News* rankings, which are then turned back to validate themselves. Due to a poor response rate from college officials, the magazine recently added high school guidance counselors to the poll for the categories of national universities and national liberal arts colleges. The response rate there has yet to reach 15 percent.

Acceptance rate, one of the problem areas susceptible to "creative" reporting, is another category that shouldn't be in the formula to begin with. The operating principle is that the lower the acceptance rate, the higher the quality. But what's important is the composition of the class that has been assembled and not what was discarded in the process. Would we rate the quality of a company's personnel by how many people they didn't hire? Or an athletic team by how many players it cut in tryouts? If management can assemble a strong team year after year from a limited pool (perhaps because those who stand no chance are not encouraged to apply) – why should they be penalized in the ratings? This point applies especially (but not only) to science and engineering schools, which commonly accept a large percentage of their applicants but have average SAT scores noticeably higher than schools of other types with comparable acceptance rates.

Alumni donation rate is another part of the schema that doesn't belong. Meant to measure alumni satisfaction with their college experience, this statistic is more likely to reflect a school's persistence at dunning. Some colleges are known to ask unabashedly for contributions as small as a dollar by saying their purpose is to bolster their rankings. Further, this category puts public institutions at a distinct disadvantage – because of their government funding, they have less need than their private counterparts to maximize alumni giving, and alumni, knowing this, feel less responsibility to give.

Three measures that are not irrelevant but that work from mistaken assumptions are the percentage of faculty who are full-time, freshman retention rate, and graduation rate. For all of them the assumption is made that 100 percent is the most desirable number, and the higher the number the better. In reality, faculties can offer students a stronger slate of courses when part-timers are brought in to teach their specialties and to counteract the problem of dead wood. Trying to determine the "best" percentage would be

impossible, but certainly it isn't 100 percent. Likewise with retention and graduation rates. Nearly perfect scores (no one reports
100 percent) may indicate that a college's grading is too easy and
that the school is afraid to wash out students who deserve it, and
that by sheer luck no one left due to ill health, to get married, to
work for a dot com, or to travel. And it may mean there is no room
to consider transfer applicants who could bring a refreshing element to the student body.

Three more measures that are relevant but misleading are
student/faculty ratio, percentage of classes with enrollment over
50, and percentage of classes with enrollment under 20. What
U.S. News is trying to get at is the amount of contact students
have with the professors who teach them. This is important, but
how should it be determined? A student/faculty ratio of less
than 10 to 1 appears impressive on paper, but if many of the
faculty are researchers who seldom teach undergraduates, the
reality may be the equivalent of 20 to 1. Conversely, in a ratio
of 15 to 1, professors may make themselves readily available. A
better measure here would be the number of hours per week
faculty spend with students, not only in class but also outside
of class in their offices. As for class size, smaller is better – this
principle works. But what needs to be determined is roughly
what percentage of a student's degree program comprises high-
enrollment courses. At some schools the number can easily run
to 35 percent or more – schools where the basic courses in most
disciplines that are taken for the first two years come in the form
of large lectures. There may be many small enrollment courses
to choose from later on in the major, so that U.S. News reports
only 10 to 15 percent of courses on the schedule enroll more
than 50. What it fails to say is that the ones over 50 get a large
share of the overall enrollment, and that most students will end
up with far more than 10 to 15 percent of their degree programs
in over-50 classes.

Still another measure that goes awry is financial resources, defined as average spending per student. The problem is that *U.S. News* includes spending not only for instructional activity, the heart of what an academic institution is all about, but for research, student services, public service, institutional support, and operations and maintenance. And it averages spending for graduate students in with undergraduates, when the rankings are supposed to be for undergraduate programs only. This kitchen-sink approach rewards schools for their wealth per se rather than how well they use it to educate students in bachelor's-degree programs.

Institutional wealth shows up improperly again in the measure of faculty salaries. Salary is a poor proxy for quality of teaching. Higher salaries at many institutions go to top researchers more than to top teachers, muddying the economic principle that high pay generates better quality work. Other factors that make this measure dubious are that some colleges may give generous salaries to full-time faculty but employ fewer of them along with more adjuncts (*U.S. News* measures salary only for full-timers), religiously affiliated colleges often draw faculty with special commitments who accept lower than average salaries, and the oversupply of qualified faculty in various subject areas means that colleges can get good teachers without paying top dollar.

Beyond the faults of the categories themselves is the problem of weighting. How much should each category and each measure within a category be worth in the overall formula? Why is student selectivity (acceptance rate, class rank, and SAT scores combined) worth 15 percent while graduation and retention rates count for 20 percent (at national universities and liberal arts colleges) or 25 percent (at master's and baccalaureate schools)? Why are financial resources 10 percent and class size 8 percent? There is no rational justification for why any factor measured is given a particular weight. Yet even a small change in the weighting would result in changes of rank for at least a few schools, and a major weight redistribution could shake things up dramatically. The highly arbitrary nature of the ranking system shows through again. The weighting is fixed, just as the categories are fixed, and not even by experts on higher education. The people setting the formula are in the business of selling magazines. In fairness to *U.S. News*, it should be noted that any rating system created by any party could be subject to the charge of arbitrariness – what counts and how much it counts in assessing the worth of something are in the end matters of judgment. But given the magazine's self-assumed mantle of authority, along with the facts that its primary objective is marketing and its methodology is opposed by a large segment of the constituency being measured, the problem of arbitrariness looms large.

Overall there is more wrong than there is right about the ranking approach *U.S. News* uses. What should be done? The magazine can't be expected to perform a major overhaul on the system that has brought it large profits for two decades. It answers to the success of its sales and not to critiques showing its faults. Neither will an anti-ranking approach do – trying to move beyond ranking and toward (or back to) merely presenting information about schools while leaving comparisons to the readers. College rankings are more popular today than ever. *U.S. News* has inspired a growing worldwide movement in which many countries now put out their own national rankings, and there are international rankings as well. And for the American public, to be denied a way to rank colleges would be considered a deprivation, since so many other things from beaches to hospitals to refrigerators are assessed this way. While it can easily be said that our society is too conscious of the status conferred by sometimes spurious and silly rankings, with so many competing products available it's only natural to want to compare them. And not only natural, it's wise to want to know where to find top quality. To suggest that such assessments are undesirable is to fall into the relativist trap that disdains the notion of excellence as being prejudicial and an enemy of equality. To deny that an assessment can be done in a fair way is another matter, but the weakness of U.S. News's approach shouldn't taken as the final word.

ALTERNATIVES

The way to deal with the deficiencies of U.S. News is not to fight the notion of ranking, but to come up with a better ranking system. Some guidebooks group schools into several tiers (usually based on selectivity in admissions) rather than giving each school an individual numerical rank. This approach makes sense, since it avoids creating separations based on small differences that are inconsequential. But it's exactly the greater precision that is missing, and that is found in U.S. News, that commands the public's attention as they try to sort through the vast number of American colleges. Numerical rankings are here to stay. Taking that as a given, how should a formula be constructed that does better than the highly flawed one that produces annual best sellers? What categories should be included?

There's been no shortage of answers, as both educational organizations and commercial publications have tried their hand. The key for several of them has been to emphasize the outcomes of a college education rather than the capabilities of the students as they enter or the resources institutions have. Some reformists have suggested using the opinions of students nearing graduation about the education they've received, based on the National Survey of Student Engagement (NSSE) that many colleges already participate in. Another suggestion has been to use the results from the Collegiate Learning Assessment (CLA), a test of critical thinking that rates freshmen and seniors on reading a set of materials and writing a summary memo or position statement. One think tank has proposed a formula combining these factors with a third one of success after graduation as determined by employment earnings and entrance into graduate school.

A much different system was created by *Washington Monthly* magazine. The emphasis here is on the graduation rate of students with Pell grants, an institution's research capabilities, and "service" as shown in how many graduates enter the Peace Corps or the military. *Forbes* has taken its turn at college rankings by featuring alumni and faculty awards, student evaluations of professors on RateMyProfessors.com, and student debt at graduation. *Kiplinger's* has rated public colleges only, using some of *U.S. News's* categories, combined with the factors of cost and financial aid, to give a best-for-your-money result.

Efforts like these underscore the point that ranking systems can be devised that are very different from the one used by *U.S. News*. But are they better? Assessing outcomes is a good idea – certainly we want to know about the quality of the graduates colleges turn out. However, outcome assessments have strong drawbacks. They're very difficult to carry out with the precision needed to make a formal ranking system inclusive and fair. The rate of participation is problematic. For NSSE it includes fewer than half of the roughly 1,500 institutions on the *U.S. News* list, and for CLA it's about 15 percent. When a survey method is used such as with NSSE, or to get other information such as alumni employment or attendance in graduate school, the response rate typically is low, and if the survey involves opinions, the ones it draws may not be representative. When dealing with alumni, simply obtaining contact information is difficult, no less getting them to reply to survey questions. It's possible that NSSE could be administered to all seniors as they take final exams, but many colleges would likely back off out of fear of the results if they knew they'd be compared with other colleges. And some might find ways to game the results.

With actual assessments of learning such as CLA, or, as some have suggested, the GRE, getting high participation faces even tougher going. Again, if the results are to be used comparatively, colleges will resist out of worry about how their students will perform, and students will object to an added academic burden. Mandated testing would lead to massive test prep programs and questions of statistical validity because of them, and possibly to legal challenges. Exit testing, then, faces the prospect of considerable opposition, which, coupled with the liabilities of surveys, means the outcome assessments that reformists want to see across the full range of colleges are not likely to be done in the near future. Unless or until valid assessment outcomes are devised and accepted, creating an alternative to *U.S. News* will have to get along without them.

When putting together a new formula, there's a tendency found among some of *U.S. News*'s critics, and some of the competing magazine rankings, that needs to be avoided. That tendency is to replace measures like the reputational poll, financial resources, and faculty salaries, which are steeped in public relations and institutional wealth, with features that key on social consciousness, such as financial aid, the performance of low income students, and "service" performed by students or an institution generally. In other words, class bias favoring the more fortunate gives way to class bias favoring the less fortunate. A tendency toward class bias in either direction should be held in check. It distracts attention from the primary function of institutions of higher education, which is not to confer status and not to make up for a lack of it. The primary function is to provide an academic learning experience, and this is what should be measured. It's the availability of this experience that a ranking system should focus on.

The three main factors that determine this experience are students, faculty, and curriculum. These are the categories that should compose a new ranking formula. It's the quality of each that is in question. Students with a high level of academic preparation, intellectual curiosity, and desire to excel allow professors to demand a high level of performance. And they help to create an overall campus atmosphere of seriousness about learning – strong students push each other intellectually in daily conversation. The two key measures in this category should be scores on the SAT or ACT and high-school GPA or rank in class. Classroom performance, while subject to wide variances among individual high schools over the difficulty of their coursework, gives a helpful picture of a college's student body overall when the figures are rolled together into an average. The standardized tests provide the only common measure of all students, the only means for comparing them all on the same basis. To avoid giving a bump to "test optional" schools, their average scores should be discounted by the percentage of their students who didn't submit scores.

Another possible consideration is the performance of students in their college studies, but a fair comparative assessment is difficult. To rate schools on the basis of their students' GPAs would be an open invitation for grade inflation and make a problem they're fighting against today even more serious. So that measure wouldn't work. If retention and graduation rate are used to measure academic performance as *U.S. News* does, the percentage measurements should be loosened. Rather than assuming mistakenly that 100 percent retention is optimal, and measuring schools on a point-by-point basis up to it, a set of thresholds could be established at 10 percent intervals. In this way, 90 percent or more might receive maximum credit for freshman retention, and perhaps 80 percent for graduation rate.

The second main category to be assessed is the quality of the faculty. Their importance is obvious for their function of conveying the curriculum to the students. They shouldn't be rated for their research and publishing, since this is a different function from teaching, and although it's sometimes claimed that doing research makes for good teaching, there are many excellent teachers who do little of it, and also top researchers who are known as weak teachers. Two factors *U.S. News* uses that are significant are the percentage of faculty who are full-time and the percentage with the highest degree in their field. But in both cases leeway should be given for having a few good people who stand outside the profile – ones whose extensive experience or special expertise allows a school to strengthen its teaching overall. Taking this flexibility into consideration, a threshold of perhaps 80 to 90 percent should be worth the highest rating, with continuing downward intervals of 10 percent each rather than single digits at 1 percent. Beyond this, a means should be established to factor in (negatively) the use of graduate assistants, who are part-time and without terminal degrees or much experience, but who in some accounts are classified as students rather than as faculty and thus hidden from view. The real question to be gotten at is not the percentage of faculty per se who are full-time or fully credentialed, but the percentage of students' time in teaching situations that is spent with teachers who have these qualifications.

The strategy of revealing where students' time is spent can also be applied to class size. Instead of focusing on what percentage of courses have enrollments of less than 20 or more than 50 (the *U.S. News* standards), what needs to be determined is how much of a student's degree program is spent in large classes versus how much is in small classes. Also very important about time is how much of it faculty make available to undergraduate students outside of the classroom. Colleges might complain if they're asked to provide this kind of data, but it could be added to the Common Data Set questionnaire they already fill out annually for use by the various guidebooks. The process of data collection will involve added work, but accomplishing it isn't an unreasonable expectation for the institutional-research personnel that colleges employ.

The main problem won't be in whether colleges want to cooperate, but in determining whether the data they submitted should be counted on as accurate or suspected of being inflated.

Between students and faculty lies the curriculum. In assessing a college for the quality of the academic experience it offers, the matter of what students are learning is as important as who's learning it and who's teaching it. Neither *U. S. News* nor its competitors factor this into their rankings, yet the main accrediting agencies find the curriculum important enough to be included when they review colleges, even if they tend to be lenient in interpreting what they find. The curriculum is the great unknown that has been left out of college rankings and needs to be included. Measuring it will be time consuming, and subject to controversy over what constitutes high quality and what doesn't, but the prospect is feasible.

Rating the upper-level curriculum where students take their majors would be especially complicated and difficult, since it would involve an analysis of the full course list for each department within a college, and departments from different colleges have different strengths and specializations. General education, on the other hand, encompasses fewer courses and is more easily subject to comparisons among institutions. Here is where the ratings should focus. The needed information can be drawn from the catalogs and course schedules available on college websites.

Fields such as engineering and the arts (conservatory-type degrees) traditionally have attempted only the bare minimum of 30 semester credits of general education the accrediting agencies require, and a dispensation for this fact can be built in when developing a rating system. Otherwise, the system can ask about how extensive the general education requirements are, how well organized, and whether specialized courses are allowed to count as general education. Mere bulk in course choices or required credits shouldn't be accepted as outweighing a solid, well-justified set of courses. Beyond a college's established requirements is the question of what courses are actually offered – are there enough sections or seats available in basic courses, or do students have to scramble to fit those courses into their schedules or else take obscure offerings instead? Also important is the matter of who teaches the general education courses, and at this point rating the curriculum dovetails with rating the faculty. To what extent are the basic courses taught by regular full-time faculty, and to what extent by graduate students, part-timers, and temporary faculty?

A good model for rating general education programs already exists. In 2009 the American Council of Trustees and Alumni, a national higher-education reform organization, launched WhatWillTheyLearn.com, and since then general education at more than 1000 schools has been examined by using information available on their websites. Schools are graded A through F according to how many of seven basic subjects students are required to take – foreign language to show competency at the intermediate level, and at least one course each in composition, literature, U.S. government or history, economics, mathematics, and natural science. Broad-based, survey-type courses count, specialized ones don't. With sufficient time and staff, this online college guide could expand to include as many schools as *U.S. News*, and to consider who does the teaching in general education, whether some of the schools go further than requiring the seven basic courses, and whether their master schedules make the courses easily available for students.

The system proposed here is based on the idea of quality in academics, using only measures that relate to it fundamentally and directly. It avoids the superficiality of peer assessment and the favoritism toward institutional wealth that are found in *U.S. News*. It also avoids using measures found in other ranking systems, such as cost of attendance, financial aid, and percentage of graduates entering "service" fields, that fail to speak to academic quality, as well as measures where obtaining comprehensive data is unfeasible. In spite of these improvements over other systems, a major concern remains. The categories are fixed. It might be that someone agrees with them for the most part but would like to add or subtract a bit, and just as with the other systems, this is impossible. The consumer of the data is stuck with their finality. The same goes for the weighting the categories have been given – whatever that is, it can be seen as arbitrary and beyond control. Even if this system is better than the others, it can still be seen as sharing with them the critical feature of inflexibility. In that sense it adds another ranking system to a list that includes *U.S. News* along with several others. This helps to point out that ranking systems are indeed plural, and that the supposed leader is only one among several alternatives, each with its own rigidity. But it will also leave many people wanting more.

What's missing, but within reach using recent computer technology, is the opportunity for college watchers to customize the rankings as they see fit. Personalized college-finder websites are already available in which users select a combination of categories such as test score level, size of the student body, and location, to produce a list of schools meeting their criteria. This sort of technology could be applied to a system of ranking. The new system could offer online not only the original version of itself as determined by its formula, but the opportunity to add or subtract categories, as well as to change their weightings. While the original may be defended on both philosophical and practical terms, individuals with their own ideas about what counts most and least could impose their will on it. In addition to the categories of the new system, the data used in other ranking systems, including *U.S. News*, could be made available in a smorgasbord of mix and match (While the magazines hold the rights to what they publish, they don't have exclusive use of the data, and it can be drawn from other sources.) For instance, someone could use the formula from the new system as a base but change the category weighting and add data about cost of attendance and acceptance rate. Simply pressing a button would make a customized ranking list appear. Or maybe the curriculum category from the new formula would be dropped, or SAT scores, with CLA test results added (for the limited number of schools willing to participate in having their scores listed). A different customized list would result.

While anyone researching colleges would benefit from the flexible online ranking system, high school guidance counselors especially would find it helpful. It supports the idea many of them emphasize about choosing a college for its "fit" rather than for the prestige it carries. Prestige as designated by a ranking number becomes variable with the scrambling of computerized data. The availability of customized rankings should give the lie once and for all to the notion that *U.S. News* can tell us which schools are better than others. The answer depends on the type of data being considered, and the type of data would become the choice of individuals and not the preference of magazine editors.

The Prestige Factor

The *U.S. News* college rankings have grown to their present level of importance because they're driven by a major underlying force. What the magazine's sales depend on is public opinion about the worth of attending a top college. When people compare schools, they're interested in the quality of the learning experience that's available, but they're often especially conscious of the prestige that attaches to certain names. The commonly accepted view is that holding a degree from a prominent institution confers an advantage in life, that it spells success in a continuing and most important way.

Prior to the 20th century mere attendance at college separated a person from the crowd. It wasn't necessary to complete a degree, and often that wasn't the goal, in order to achieve high educational status. During the century, as going to college became more common, the respected sign of attainment rose to be possession of a bachelor's degree. And in the last several decades, with many people now holding degrees, increasing attention has been given to which colleges they come from. While attendance at certain well-known schools was always held in high regard, only in recent times has it come to be seen by many as invaluable for success. The economic principle that value derives from scarcity has led many consumers of higher education to put special emphasis on the name and ranking of a college as representing the worth of studying there. *U.S. News* derives its popularity from this attitude, and then reinforces it by evoking an aura of exclusivity for a limited number of schools.

What, then, does the prestige factor consist of? What does it represent that's thought to be so advantageous? For some believers there's a personal or social expectation. Being educated at a top school carries an air of intellectual and cultural superiority. It's associated with elevated thinking and sophistication. All of this fits nicely into maintaining high social class or as a means for rising to that level. But this image has a counterpart with an undesirable taint that is probably at least as well recognized. Intellectuality may come off as egg-headedness or pretentiousness, and being out of touch with the realities of everyday life. The social ramification is snobbery blended with a sense of entitlement, something many people find off-putting. This mixed review suggests that it isn't the personal or social factors associated with a prestigious education that account for its strong demand.

What does account for it is identification with professional gain. Preparing for the job world is broadly held to be the paramount aim of a college education, and with it goes the idea that the best in the job world is connected with the best of educational institutions. Several interrelated beliefs are involved here – a big-time diploma makes it easier to become a doctor, attorney, entre-preneur, scientist, engineer, or politician, and easier to rise to the top within these fields. It's considered a leg up for getting into graduate schools, especially the best graduate schools. For college grads when they're looking for work, it's said that employers are impressed with credentials from leading institutions, and they give preference in hiring to students who have gone there. Especially in getting the first job, coming from a highly reputed school is hailed as a boost. Beyond that, one perspective sees a diminishing return in hiring as someone's career moves along, while another perspec-tive asserts that top schools have well developed alumni networks that will take care of their own throughout their careers. Overrid-ing any confusion that might result between these perspectives is a confidence that over all, through the course of a lifetime, graduates of prestigious colleges will show their colors by out-earning those of other colleges.

Unfortunately for the people who pursue this idealized notion of a prestigious college degree, it's highly flawed, consisting partly of myth and partly of misunderstanding. While graduates of lead-ing schools often enter the most respected professions, there are many more graduates from other colleges who do so as well. And many of the latter rise to the top – the very top. Consider the back-grounds of business executives. A 2006 study of the CEOs of the Fortune top 50 companies showed that 20 came from Ivy League schools and other schools on the lists of top 50 universities and top 50 liberal arts colleges reported by *U.S. News*. But the other 30 came from institutions not on those lists. With politicians we find a similar pattern. Among our nation's governors and members of the House and Senate of the U.S. Congress, about two thirds did not attend colleges on either of the top-50 lists. Clearly it's some-thing other than where they went to college that separated these business and political leaders from the crowd and spelled success for them in achieving a high position.

What about financial advantage, the notion that the prestige of the college a person attends relates to earnings potential? Various surveys have shown that graduates from the foremost colleges, on average, earn more money than those from other schools. This much isn't in dispute. However, it's an unsubstantiated leap to assume that the status of the college attended is actually a cause for the earnings differential. What a definitive study has revealed is that graduates of other colleges whose high school records equal those from elite schools are on a par with them in earnings. Over the duration of their careers they earn just as much. Whatever accounts for the success of the highest earners, it doesn't consist of having attended a big-name college. And even with getting a first job, the supposed connection turns out to be less than degree holders from top schools might hope for. A 2008 survey of 500 top entry-level employers found that when college grads try to get their foot in the door, the people on the other side are more interested in their major, their interviewing skills, and their internship experience than the name of the college they attended. Coming from a highly reputed school may help, but only if other more important conditions have been met.

If the earning power of a diploma from a prominent institution has been overestimated, what about the value of an alumni network? Having the connections it offers is a plus, but there are reasons to question how much that plus amounts to. Many colleges have well developed alumni networks – leading names are far from the only ones. Prestigious U may have its loyal graduates, but Semi-Prestigious U and Non-Prestigious U do as well. With today's technology and the ways young people apply it in their gregarious habits, it's now easy to make the connections that once were the province of well-oiled alumni associations. And the same expertise and behavior that encourage connections among college alumni work for other groups as well. High schools have well-developed alumni networks, fraternities and sororities have national networks, and corporations over the past couple of decades have made much use of networks of former workers they call their "alumni." Then there are the graduate and professional school networks that may be more important than the undergraduate ones for professional success. With all of the networking available, how important in the large scheme of career advancement is the kind that's done through college alumni, whether it's with a big-name school or any other school? While the help is there, what it amounts to is one more way of making career connections among several others.

The remaining claim about the benefit of going to an elite college is that it's an asset for getting into graduate school. After all, in many fields students don't stop with a bachelor's degree – graduate-level training is a must. Is the connection that's assumed between a having prestigious diploma and graduate school admission real? The answer is a cautionary maybe – in some cases it may give a boost. However, the caution is that in other cases it may be a drawback.

Graduate programs typically emphasize that the most important factors in admissions are grade point average, standardized test scores, and reference letters. Job experience also counts. The reputation of an applicant's college may be a factor, but a degree from a highly ranked school won't make up for a low test score (GRE, LSAT, GMAT, MCAT) or weak grades. Admissions committees are quick to say they're looking for strong applicants from a broad range of colleges. On the other hand, profiles posted by some of the most notable graduate programs show that often a majority of their students come from leading undergraduate colleges, although a significant number come from lesser-known institutions. It might be tempting to conclude that having a big-name diploma is an advantage, at least at the top tier of graduate schools, but the phenomenon involved may be similar to what was found with earnings – sharp students, regardless of where they come from, stand out. Prominent colleges draw a disproportionately large number of them from the high school population to their undergraduate programs and turn them out four years later ready for graduate school. Students at other colleges who have capabilities equal to their prestige-carrying colleagues also seem to fare well in graduate admissions, but the number of them coming from any one institution tends to be significantly fewer than the number coming from one of the top-ranked schools.

Given the above picture, there are several reasons why not attending an elite college may be advantageous for getting into graduate school. The competition for grades in an elite setting will be much greater. Most of the students were high school stars, but every second one will graduate from college in the bottom half of their class, not a helpful factor when admissions committees take a look. And the GPA and ranking numbers may be influential in another way – as a drain on confidence and desire. Former stars who grade out as merely mediocre (or less than that) lose out on the enjoyment that goes with academic accomplishment, and their drive to excel may suffer. Someone with the capability to do good graduate work may choose not to try, or may need a few years of ego repair before being ready.

For some students the damage may be even greater because lack of success dissuaded them from pursuing a major they truly desired. This happens especially in the natural sciences, where a student gives up a dream to be a doctor or physicist, not out of lack of ability, but because of a level of competition that weeds out the good in favor of the best, something far less likely to happen at a school of lesser stature. There a good student will pursue any major and will find high grades reasonably within reach, along with the positive attitude that goes with accomplishment and confidence about moving on to the next level. This student has a much better chance to stand out from the crowd rather than a risk of getting lost in it.

A summary of the cautionary maybe about the worth a degree from a leading college carries in graduate school admission says there should be an advantage for a student with a strong academic record. But one who has done poorly would have been better off, and one in the middle might have been, attending a less prominent school and taking advantage of the less intense competition so as to be at the top academically and to feel confident and eager to go on. This situation combines with the facts that the majority of top professionals don't come from top-ranked colleges and that graduates of those colleges earn no more than their intellectual counterparts from other schools, along with reservations about the worth of alumni networking relative to other kinds of networking – to tell us that the advantage of holding a prestigious diploma is at least as much fantasy as it is reality. While it may gain attention and be a plus up to a point, it's neither essential for success nor an assurance of it. People who understand this are unlikely to be enamored with the featured names in *U.S. News*. Those who have been smitten by the prospect of prestige would do well to reevaluate its worth.

3

AFFIRMATIVE ACTION
AND ELUSIVE EQUALITY

Should minority students get preference in college admissions? Legacies and athletes do, and while colleges are criticized for the practice, the struggle is considerably less than with the firestorm of legal activity and moral sentiment that swirls around special breaks for minorities. As the controversy has intensified, minority preference has become enmeshed with preference for the other two groups. When criticism is leveled against affirmative action, its supporters often say that since legacies and athletes benefit from favoritism, then minorities should too. The charge is that it's hypocritical and unfair to bend the standards for the other groups without doing it for minorities. Preferences have come to be seen as a collective enterprise where entitlement for one group is used to justify entitlement for another.

The problem with this way of thinking is that the groups are not at all alike. Each has its own essential nature. They're defined by different traits. And the reasons colleges have for wanting their presence on campus are different for each group. So consideration of whether the groups should be given preference should take place for each group individually. What holds for one shouldn't be assumed to hold for another.

Minority preference is the only one of the three that points toward the fundamental purpose of higher education institutions – learning. Diversity is heralded as important for widening the range of thinking students are exposed to both inside and outside the classroom. Athletes, in contrast, get preference so colleges can enliven their extracurricular activities and provide entertainment for sports fans, and with legacies the main goal is fundraising. In minority preference the defining group trait is race or ethnicity. Affirmative action is for black and Hispanic students (and in their small numbers, Native Americans) – groups that are underrepresented at selective schools, where they lose out in straight-up competition with whites and Asians. The defining trait here is very different than it is with athletes, where it's a talent, and with legacies, where it's a family connection. Athletes can choose not to continue using their athletic talent, and legacies lose their edge by applying to any school other than where their family went. But for minorities, the group trait carries with them wherever they go – it can't be discontinued or forfeited. They may choose not to emphasize it and not to use it as a hook in college admissions, but it doesn't go away. It's something that remains always, and for many people it's visible whether they prefer it to be or not.

The nature of minority status runs deeper than the nature of the other two groups, and its potential effect is more important. Affirmative action carries a noble inspiration to improve our society, while preference for legacies and athletes does not. Minority preference addresses a fundamental moral issue that has plagued our nation throughout its existence. The success or failure of the means colleges use to deal with the issue looms large not only as a measure of the schools themselves, but also as a model for institutions outside of higher education to follow.

Compensatory Justice and Diversity

The purpose of minority preference is twofold. The original argument was for compensatory justice – to make up for the unequal opportunity minorities have faced in access to higher education. They've endured slavery, segregation, sweatshops, migrant labor camps, and social prejudice, which have translated into low income, substandard housing, and inadequate primary and secondary schooling, so they shouldn't be expected to be performing at as high a level academically as the white population. The fair and proper thing to do is give them a chance to catch up by offering access to the top colleges their conditions have precluded them from attending.

While compensatory justice is still very much on the minds of affirmative action advocates, today the argument more often heard for minority preference is that it's for the purpose of enhancing the educational experience college students undergo. The key word is "diversity." Having a racially diverse student body prepares students to live in a pluralistic society. It helps to diminish prejudice and discrimination by making them more familiar with and more respectful of the diverse groups that make up our society outside of higher education. The idea is that familiarity breeds understanding and is the basis for groups accepting one another on equal footing. Familiarity comes when minorities voice viewpoints different from those of other people, and when they display cultural practices particular to their groups. Equal footing comes when it's seen that minorities have something worthwhile to say, and that they're as capable as other people at intellectual labor and of qualifying for graduate study and entering professional positions.

An extension of the diversity argument is angled toward leadership. Developing leaders of varied racial and ethnic backgrounds is important. In a well functioning society, blacks and Hispanics will hold leadership positions in all aspects of the society.

Affirmative action is needed to ensure that a fair share of minority leaders are trained, and that minority concerns are spoken for in a strong voice that has a true grasp of those concerns.

Various criticisms have emerged against the purpose of compensatory justice as well as against that of diversity. A cynical view says compensatory justice is for whites who feel "white guilt" and are trying to atone for it. The idea is that their concern is for doing something to help themselves, and that helping minorities is merely a condition to be dealt with in finding the way to a clear conscience. While the feeling of guilt the critics speak of may be real, this accusation is off target. Sometimes it's put in a way that makes supporters of minority preference seem calculating. The insinuation is that they're conscious that affirmative action is harmful rather than helpful, but they still want to pursue it for the self-serving reason that it makes them feel good. But that notion is dubious. Would they feel good if they knew the preference was harmful and they were still supporting it for selfish reasons? A less pointed interpretation assumes that the guilt and atonement are subconscious, but nevertheless self-centered. What's implied is a confused mind with an overactive conscience. For some people this may be the case, but the role of conscience shouldn't be dismissed. In the realm of morality, feelings of guilt are a powerful factor in leading people to do the right thing. Conscience is both other-directed and self-directed. The involvement of guilt and atonement shouldn't be thought of as inappropriate. All of this isn't to say the emotional experience has no downside. Even if it's well-meaning, it may hinder giving fair consideration to the negative effects that can result from preference. Emotional investment in wanting to do the right thing may weigh against a rational determination of what the right thing is. But it doesn't make sense to disrespect the legitimate role of conscience by assuming it to be only or mainly self-directed.

Another critical view says the people who are truly due compensation are not the ones that minority preference is aimed at. And the people paying the compensation are not the guilty ones. While our nation has a history of unfairness toward minorities, many changes have been made and great strides have been taken. Today's students aren't responsible for the discrimination of the past. Compensation may have been due in the past, but it isn't now for the people it affects. This view treats compensatory justice as a simple matter of reparation for prior wrongs, and it's true that people today did not cause those wrongs. But it fails to recognize that historical conditions influence the present. While preferences won't repair history, they aim to help students in the present who have had lesser opportunity because the unfair treatment dealt to their ancestors left succeeding generations wanting. Compensation for minority students is based on their lesser position in the scheme of things due to the effect of past racist practices, and a carry-through of prejudice that still exists although to a lesser degree than before.

This response, of course, presumes that the minority students being helped actually are in a lesser position than other students, that they've lived in disadvantaged conditions compared with the white and Asian students they're given preference over. But, in fact, that often isn't the case. Many students admitted under affirmative action programs, at least at the most selective colleges, come from middle and upper middle class families where their economic and social status, including access to the best schools, lies above that of many white and Asian students who lose out to them. Critics point out that the preference these students receive isn't deserved. They're given compensation for a situation that isn't theirs. While their skin color or surname classifies them as minorities, they've lived their lives absent the disadvantage that preference is meant to address.

When advantaged minority students are given preference, compensatory justice is shooting wide of its intended mark. The critics who say so are on solid ground. Still, that doesn't mean the argument should be abandoned. Compensatory justice is intended to answer a grievous and overarching wrong, one that still exists even if to a lesser degree than in the past. If while aiming to compensate those who are deserving, preference also goes toward some who are not deserving, there are still two lines of defense. One is that we can be asked to put up with some spillover of compensation in the interest of a noble good. The difficulty is that critics believe the spillover is considerable, and they haven't been disproved. The other option is to find ways to prevent the spillover and give compensation selectively to people who warrant it.

The purpose of compensatory justice isn't done in by detractors who see it as psychological "feel good" for whites, or as a misdirected correction for wrongs of the past, although these complaints have merit. And it isn't done in by failing to set boundaries to separate advantaged minorities from those who are disadvantaged. While this last point is a major devil in the details, it isn't overwhelming, and the power of compensatory justice as a moral principle remains.

Whatever its moral strength, though, the idea of compensation is on shaky ground today as a legal principle to support minority preferences. In the Supreme Court's historic Bakke v. University of California case in 1978, Justice Powell's majority opinion turned that principle aside as failing to meet a standard of "strict scrutiny." At the same time, Powell endorsed the diversity rationale by saying that promoting an optimal learning situation constitutes a "compelling societal interest" that can justify admissions preference. While the notion of diversity wasn't born with Bakke, afterward it became the lawful justification for affirmative action admissions. It remains that way after the Court's decision in the Grutter v. Bollinger case in 2003. Critics today look back at this sequence of events and assert that diversity has become a smokescreen for what really drives minority preference, which is still compensatory justice. Preference supporters, they believe, are wily enough to be quiet about their main concern and to emphasize what puts them on established legal ground, especially because preference has continued to cause legal controversy.

Criticism of the purpose of diversity often begins here – with suspicion that its proponents only believe in it halfheartedly. But is the suspicion correct? While it may have been the case that when preference advocates began proclaiming for diversity they didn't hold it as a firmly fixed vision, that isn't the case today. Many college officials and committees have issued statements about the importance of diversity, helping it to take on weight to the point of often being assumed, without discussion, to be a main goal of higher education. In fact, many preference advocates today are too young to remember Bakke, and the diversity argument is what they know as the grounding for their belief.

Simply looking historically at the rise of the diversity argument isn't enough to impugn the belief its advocates hold in it today. But critics go further, making subtler and deeper charges. They sometimes suspect advocates, especially younger ones, may not believe the purpose of diversity can truly be fulfilled. They've grown up in a society structured around preference yet where minorities continue to lag considerably behind whites in intellectual accomplishment, and where minorities and whites often opt for social separation from each other. These advocates may not think the goal of social harmony with equal accomplishment and equal respect among groups is achievable, however desirable it may be. So, the best that can be hoped for is a partitioned society where minorities have a piece of the pie reserved for them. They deserve their share, but in the foreseeable future and perhaps always they may need a special boost. When the thinking goes this way, it slides away from the true goal of diversity and toward an argument for justice. The form of justice may be compensatory, aiming at payback for unequal opportunity stemming from the past. Or it may be what philosophers would designate as distributive justice, holding that membership in our society at present entitles everyone to share in its benefits. The exact terms here may be of little consequence to most people, but the implications in the concepts are important. Compensatory justice redresses specific unfair conditions and is presumed to last only until those conditions have been removed. Distributive justice assumes society to be as it is, with its apportionment of awards not thought of as a temporary make-up but as a permanent right. Either way, though, the purpose of minority preference has shifted from diversity to justice.

To back up their suspicion that diversity is just a cover for another intention, critics note that the overall plan people are asked to accept is short on specifics. The program that has emerged is too general – when it's examined for details, the ones we should expect to find are lacking. The claim of the diversity argument is that putting students of different backgrounds together is educational – from the mix, they're exposed to a variety of points of view and a variety of social practices. But colleges today do nothing to ensure that the desired intellectual and social variety is present in the classroom or outside. They simply admit minority students. They don't take measures to place those students in courses where it would be helpful to have their viewpoint, and they don't place them strategically in campus housing to ensure a true mix. In fact, colleges do the opposite – they set up academic programs in minority studies, such as black studies and Hispanic studies, and special social programming and housing for minorities, all of which isolate minority students into enclaves away from the rest of the student body. And further, the colleges do nothing to ensure that the minority students who are admitted do in fact have views and lifestyles that are different than the rest of the student body.

Many black and Hispanic students have beliefs and lifestyles that mirror those of the white student population. Skin color and ethnicity are not an accurate proxy for the factors colleges claim to want minority students to bring to the campus. If colleges are serious about using minority preference toward an educational end, why do they give preference to many minority students who don't further that end?

Isn't the diversity argument, then, a smokescreen for justice, as critics say? Probably it is for some advocates, but if so, does that negate the worth of the argument itself? The purpose of diversity, even if some people don't think it's achievable, and whether or not the structure that's been put in place for it makes it achievable, stands on its own as a defensible moral principle. Who among the critics would deny that promoting a harmonious society with understanding and respect among racial and ethnic groups is desirable? And even if diversity doesn't exist alone in the minds of advocates as a justification for giving preference, but it shares the field with compensatory justice, this doesn't mean they're covering up. A believer in one can be a believer in the other. In fact, the two basic reasons for preference can be linked. The desire for fairness found in compensatory justice and the balance and cohesion sought through diversity are both reflections of a desire for equality.

The toughest point critics make – that if advocates were serious about diversity, they would design a means for achieving it beyond simply admitting minorities to the student body – has answers. Advocates may say they believe the purpose of diversity is being achieved, that preference is working acceptably without detailed micromanagement on campus. Or they may think that a detailed plan is inappropriate, that placing minority students strategically in certain classrooms and social settings deters their freedom of choice, and that screening them to see which ones actually have different beliefs and lifestyles than other students sounds too much like the thought police. It's possible to admit that something is lost by not having a detailed plan in place, but claim the overall result is still desirable. Possible doesn't mean convincing, of course. This line of explanation may be rationalization more than honest and clear thinking about the actual state of affairs on campuses today. But weak as it may be, it could be dealt with by admitting this and creating more structure to make for true diversity rather than settling for pockets of minority separation. And even without that admission and change, the purpose of diversity is not lost; it's just that its supporters are shortsighted.

The bottom line in calculating what critics say, and how advocates can respond, about diversity and justice as reasons for preference is that the reasons remain defensible. While those reasons show weaknesses when they're subjected to tough questioning, they still emerge as overriding concerns, as transcendent social imperatives. When we try to decide whether minority preference is a good thing, we don't find a negative answer in its purposes. But purposes are only part of a larger picture. We also want to know how well the purposes have been fulfilled. A full reckoning of affirmative action asks about its outcome – Has it been successful?

DOES PREFERENCE WORK?

If compensatory justice is working well, the status of minorities will be rising, closing the gap with whites. We would expect to see improvement over time, with minorities increasingly needing less preference than before as they assimilate into the populations of selective colleges. Unfortunately, after four decades of affirmative action in admissions, that hasn't happened. A large gap remains, and today it appears to be widening rather than closing. Minority high school graduates have always lagged far behind in SAT scores

– the key measurement for comparative group assessment of students' preparedness for college. In the 1970s the difference between blacks and whites was over 200 points on a 1600 point scale. During the next decade it narrowed to a bit below that benchmark but soon reversed to go a bit above it again, where it has stayed. The difference between whites and Hispanics is about 150 points. And if we look at the high end of the spectrum, the outlook is especially bleak. Among black students, slightly more than 1,000 throughout the U.S. each year score above 700 on the SAT math section, with a similar number on the verbal section. This is the level that the top 50 or so most selective colleges and universities are looking for, and over 100,000 students in the country achieve it in math, with about 80,000 on the verbal side. It's at the most selective schools that minority preference has caused the greatest stir, and admissions officers there haven't found the minority applicant pool to be growing stronger. They're still forced to dip far below the SAT range they desire in order to admit more than a tiny number of minority applicants. Even for the ones from well-heeled families, SAT scores trail by a wide margin. Affluent black students (family income over $100,000) measure lower than white students who come from the lowest income bracket (family income under $10,000).

With a system of preference in place for many years, minority high school graduates don't seem to be closing the readiness gap for college. But what happens to those students when colleges use preference to admit them? After all, it could be argued, college is where they're expected to forge ahead and close the gap. So that's where we should focus. The grades of minority students enrolled under affirmative action are poor – the majority at elite schools finish in the bottom quarter of their class. That finding is admitted in a well-known study done by prominent preference advocates. And minorities' test scores for admission to graduate school fall far short as well. The gap between blacks and whites on the GRE that students take for entry into programs in arts and sciences, engineering, and education, which has the same scoring scale as the SAT, is nearly 250 points. For Hispanics and whites it's nearly 150. The GMAT (business school), MCAT (medical school), and LSAT (law school) have their own scoring scales, but for all of them the differences in average scores for blacks and whites and for Hispanics and whites are equivalent to at least as much as they are on the SAT, or more. After four years when it's expected that minorities would be catching up to their white counterparts, they haven't. In order to be admitted to selective graduate programs, they need preference once again, sometimes more than they did to get into selective undergraduate colleges. And as soon as they begin studies at the advanced level, they run into more academic difficulty.

The experience of black students in law school is a telling example. Because of affirmative action, many are mismatched at schools where their undergraduate GPAs and LSAT scores are considerably less than those of the white students. This holds true not only for elite schools, but for the rest as well. When Tier I programs admit unqualified blacks, they take them away from Tier II programs where those students would have been a good fit. Then Tier II is forced to dip below its normal standards in order to enroll black students, and so on down the hierarchy of law schools. Because of this cascade effect, black law students in general perform poorly. A provocative and comprehensive study demonstrates just how much this holds true. It found that after the first year, half of all black law students were in the bottom tenth of their class, and three-quarters were in the bottom fifth. At graduation over 40 percent remained in the bottom tenth while less than 15 percent made the top half. Figuring in an attrition rate of 20 percent (more than double the rate for whites), and multiple attempts on the bar exam (with 80% of whites passing on the first attempt), the startling result was that less than 60 percent of the blacks who started in law school emerged as attorneys.

The weak performance of blacks on the bar exam spills over into a controversy between minority advocates and public officials in states that want to raise licensing standards for becoming a practicing attorney. When several states raised the passing exam score, while other states debated doing it and decided not to, the minority position argued that a stricter standard will disproportionately reduce the number of minority attorneys when more, not fewer, are needed. The fear is that the existing small part of the legal profession who are minorities will shrink even more. The opposing position said professional licensing should be concerned foremost with setting adequate standards for the good of the public the licensees will serve, rather than with achieving racial balance. Here, in the public eye, we see the effects of a continued achievement gap between minorities and whites – beyond admission to college and through completion of graduate school, to joining the ranks of practicing professionals.

As the controversy over licensing standards suggests, putting as many minority attorneys into practice as possible is a paramount concern for affirmative-action supporters. They recognize that an achievement gap exists between minorities and whites, but say, nevertheless, the number of minority attorneys is increasing, and this is an important outcome – preference is generating social change toward greater minority inclusion in an area where it's needed. This claim, though, is questionable. Critics counter that the system of preference is actually holding down the number of minority attorneys. Without preference there would be an increase, since students would go to law schools where their preparation matched that of the student body in general. Their grades would be better, and they'd have a better understanding of the law and greater confidence that would lead to better performance on the bar exam. The research study that detailed the achievement gap bears out this point through statistics. It found that without preference, about 15 percent fewer blacks would be admitted to law school – those who probably wouldn't get through to pass the bar exam anyway. The rest would go where they were qualified (meaning few to elite schools), and since the data show they do as well as whites in situations where their qualifications match, they would graduate and pass the bar exam at similar rates. The net result would be more black attorneys.

Another major study makes a related point about another profession. A longtime complaint about college faculties is that they lack sufficient minority members. It's been thought that when preference is given to minorities to attend elite undergraduate schools, they'll be inspired and prepared to go on to get Ph.D.s and become professors. But as with attorneys, the finding is that fewer minorities are reaching the professional goal than would reach it without preference. Earning much lower grades than whites at elite colleges, graduating minorities are more wary than whites to apply to Ph.D. programs, although when they were freshmen both groups were equally interested in a career as a professor. At a college where their academic preparation matched that of the white students, minorities would earn better grades, and be more inclined to pursue doctoral degrees and become professors.

What we learn from the experience of minorities who aspire to become attorneys and college professors is that the system of giving preference in admission is problematic. Preference creates a mismatch that sets minorities up for poor performance, which in turn can generate pressure against strengthening standards in the professions as well as dissuade minorities from entering them. In other words, not only has our several-decades-old system of minority preference failed to result in closing the gap among high school students in their readiness for competitive colleges, but the system also has failed to result in minorities' closing the gap as undergraduates, and, beyond that, at the graduate-school level. This is the situation as it can be seen from the outside, but just what is there on the inside that accounts for it. What happens so that, when minorities are given an opportunity through preference, they don't make up ground? Why does their performance continue to lag far behind whites? Some analysts are tempted to look for the answer in inferior economic circumstances, but that approach becomes dubious when it's recognized that even economically advantaged minorities do relatively poorly on standardized testing. A better explanation looks beyond economics to other elements of social science and to common sense. And it's willing to consider how failure to close the gap can occur not in spite of, but precisely because of, the system of preference.

Psychologists, sociologists, and other expert commentators have noted several factors that contribute to minorities' continued low academic performance. These factors are not mutually exclusive, but are interrelated, and they may all be influential to a greater or lesser degree. One key factor is a state of mind harboring feelings of inferiority and anxiety. Students admitted through preference know they're not as well prepared as the student body in general at their college. They become anxious about their shortcomings, which hinders their performance. It may be that nervousness causes trouble in test-taking. It may be that they use their lack of preparation as an excuse not to give full effort, as a way of fulfilling a self-prophecy. The feeling of inferiority can easily relate to a sense of victimhood, where the reason for lack of preparation is said to be society at-large, racism, and inferior opportunities for minorities. Identifying as a victim can hold someone back, inhibit development of the confidence needed to forge ahead. It not only excuses failure and lack of effort, but gives approval to it and provides comfort through a feeling of moral indignation.

A sense of victimhood may incite a desire to separate from white culture and to choose contrary ideals and behaviors. Minority students who do well at academics are sometimes chided by their peers for "acting white." Peer pressure is a key component here. Academic knowledge and excellence are associated with whites, and are held apart from the identity of being a minority. The term "acting white" is pejorative, with a message of anti-intellectualism . Intellectualism is for whites, whose culture is responsible for minority victimhood, so being a good student is rejected.

Still another factor analysts have cited for minorities' continued lag in academic performance is a lack of incentive. At a young age, minority students become aware of the system of preference in education. An understanding of it is ingrained in them. They know they can be accepted into selective schools based on lesser accomplishments than whites, and because of this they may give less than their best effort. They do what's needed to accomplish their goal, but don't go beyond. The level they have to reach is only to be the best among their own ethnic group, not best among students overall. To be best among one's own group is praiseworthy, and carries a sense of accomplishment that may push aside any feelings of guilt about slacking on effort. This attitude is sometimes referred to for blacks as the "best black syndrome." It acts as an enticement not to push for excellence in academic performance.

These four factors – feeling inferior, a sense of victimhood, separatism from "acting white," and loss of incentive – help to explain why minority students continue to lag behind whites in academic performance. They're sometimes labeled, individually or collectively, as "stereotype threat." That term sums up a mindset that dissuades students from achieving up to their potential. The mindset is noxious and needs to be eliminated. The system of minority preferences not only doesn't help to do this, but it serves as a counteracting force. It becomes a causal factor against minority performance. Preference contributes to feelings of inferiority by creating a mismatch, and opens the door to accepting victimhood and separateness as ways to duck out. And it creates an obvious disincentive for giving full effort. If minority students are ever to close the gap with whites, they need to work above the level where they are now, and to do this they need to be free of a negative mindset and the conditions that contribute to it.

The aim of compensatory justice is to eliminate barriers and give minorities a chance, to allow them to achieve in spite of a system that has discouraged it. It was clear that segregation and prejudice were barriers, and admissions preference was instituted as a response. It was expected that when minorities were given the opportunity, they would gradually catch up with whites and the need for preference would diminish. Statistics tell us the expectation is far from being met, and recognition of the negative mindset that preference feeds into tells us that preference itself acts as a barrier. The tool designed to aid compensatory justice comes back against that aim. It's time to admit that a good intention has gone awry. If achieving compensatory justice involves eliminating barriers to accomplishment, and preference has turned out to be a barrier, then it's time to eliminate preference.

The counterpart of preference as a deterrent to compensatory justice is preference as a deterrent to diversity. Not only does it contribute to a negative mindset for minorities, but also to a different kind of negative mindset for whites. A resentment has developed from knowing that minority students with lesser academic accomplishment than theirs routinely get preference over them. It's easy to draw the conclusion that minorities are intellectually inferior, and that's why they need a boost. This is the opposite of the outcome diversity aims at. Instead of fostering mutual respect, and awareness that minorities are as capable as others, preference leads to disrespect. This disrespect – the notion about intellectual capability – should not be underestimated. It's considered a taboo in our society to talk about it – it creates hostility in mixed-race company, and otherwise is avoided whenever it's thought someone present might find it distasteful. But it's the unfortunate attitude that is encouraged when people know their chances, or the chances of their relatives and friends, for attending the selective colleges and graduate schools of their choice are reduced by minority preference. This attitude is a harmful undercurrent in race relations. Supporters of affirmative action often downplay it, naively thinking diversity will overcome it. Or they show moral outrage and take it to be a continuation of old-time racial prejudice. What they fail to understand is the impact it carries, and that it's generated as a new-fashioned prejudice based on personal experience with our social system today rather than something dragged along from the past.

When the outcome of affirmative action breeds resentment and disdain toward minorities, a stigma is created that they're unable to avoid. Their competence in professional fields is questioned, if only in a whisper or even if nothing is said at all. The most obvious examples are of surgeons, pilots, leaders of military combat groups – people whose skills make a difference in situations of life and death. But the question holds for other fields as well. Minority professionals go through life facing doubts about whether they got to where they are because of preference, or because they are good. This situation is not their fault and it's beyond their control. But it exists as a legacy of preference.

The purpose of diversity is not being accomplished through preference just as the purpose of compensatory justice is not. They can't be accomplished because the system of preference isn't realistic about what happens to people who are asked to perform at a level beyond what they're prepared for. When they struggle, they'll see themselves as unequal, and others will see them that way as well. Their underperformance will continue and only deepen the suspicion that minorities are not as capable and will forever need a special break. Is there any greater factor to promote racism than to thrust minorities into a position where their performance comes up short and makes them appear incapable?

Being underprepared doesn't mean truly being incapable, but the system of preference makes it appear that way. What would happen if preference were removed and minorities were left to compete on equal footing? Their numbers at the most selective institutions would drop dramatically, but not to zero. Everyone would know that the minorities at those schools were fully prepared and capable. The impetus for a negative mindset among minorities, and among whites, would be removed, and the opportunity to build unmitigated respect would begin. Would minorities' performance improve to close the gap and qualify them in larger numbers, eventually approximating what those numbers were under preference, or more? To suggest that wouldn't happen is a reason to continue with preference, giving up on the idea that minorities truly have the capability. Otherwise, we can ask how long it will take. Certainly a few years. Perhaps a decade? Longer? Whatever the time, this step treats minorities as truly equal, giving them opportunity by removing a barrier that wasn't meant to be one but turned out to be.

The idea that preference hasn't worked is often met with resistance in light of the worthy purposes preference is meant to serve, and the fact that America's selective colleges, especially the most selective ones, have committed heavily to using it. Even when the downside of preference is taken into account, advocates point to the leadership argument as justifying what's been done and for continuing it in the future. Preference, we're told, has provided us with minority professionals who are leaders both in integrating society at-large and in strengthening the minority communities they come from. They're changing the face of the professions, and they give voice to the needs of their own people. The argument is sometimes couched in a metaphor popularized by the title of a widely read book that has been hailed as the definitive defense of affirmative action admissions – *The Shape of the River*. The river represents forward movement, and what the system has accomplished is like changing the direction of its meandering water. Its shape has been engineered to remove the bends that have slowed minority accomplishment, and allow for a stronger flow of minority talent. While acknowledging that preference has its downside, the contention is that producing leaders outweighs it, that having minority talent flowing into our society is a must.

This line of thinking is emotionally appealing but logically weak. It assumes that having minorities attend elite institutions is a necessity for producing minority professionals who will exercise leadership. That isn't the case. It's not necessary to attend an elite school in order to be a leader in business, politics, medicine, law, or any field. A simple look around our country says so. Many of our professionals – both minorities and whites – and the leaders among them come from colleges and graduate schools other than the highly selective ones. This holds even for the people at the very top – Data show that the alma maters for a large majority of Fortune 50 CEOs, governors, and members of the U.S. House of Representatives and Senate aren't found among the 100 top schools listed by *U.S. News* (the best known forum for ranking colleges). We have no reason to think that without preference, talented minorities enrolled at institutions where their preparation was a fit rather than a stretch would not be successful and be leaders.

The other problem with the leadership argument is the relative weight it gives to putting minority talent through certain institutions versus the downside of the social engineering project. It fails to recognize the degree of harm that results from the negative mindset social engineering causes and perpetuates among minorities, and from the counterpart negative mindset among whites. The leadership argument underestimates the significance of the stigma minority professionals are forced to bear, and, generally, doesn't see how limited its insight has become in order to claim to be promoting progress. To continue the chosen metaphor, it's too caught up in shifting the water flow to look below the surface. The unfortunate lesson we should have learned by now is that it's a mistake to change the shape of the river when the water is poisoned in the process.

STAND-INS FOR AFFIRMATIVE ACTION

Amidst mounting criticism and legal battling about the use of preference, two replacement plans have emerged in recent years that have gained national attention. Both intend to help minorities get into selective colleges they don't qualify for directly, but without admissions offices giving them a break because of their race. One is the percentage plan, in which a fixed percentage of students from each high school graduating class in a given state qualifies for admission at the state's selective public colleges – based on grade point average alone (without SAT scores). Florida, Texas, and California authored this approach with 20 percent, 10 percent, and 4 percent plans respectively. Private colleges are not bound by this system, and haven't initiated it on their own.

On the surface, percentage plans are a populist measure that treats all high schools equally – affluent or poor, high achieving or low achieving – and is race neutral. Disadvantaged students of all races will have opportunity if they're in the top part of their class. In truth, though, the plans were designed with race very much in mind. They were implemented to counteract legal prohibitions set in place by state government or the courts against employing racial preference. The plans are really a surrogate means for ensuring that minority students are admitted in significant numbers to selective colleges. In all three states there are numerous high schools with high concentrations of minority students, which assures that many of the top qualifiers from those schools will be black and Hispanic. This is not to say the percentage approach couldn't be advocated in states without de facto segregated schools. To do that would maintain a populist purpose of sorts but without emphasizing race. No states seem interested.

Is the purpose of the percentage plans a worthy one? To the extent that it acts as a disguise, its moral standing could be questioned. But the underlying impetus – the continuance of what racial preference had intended in putting minority students into selective colleges – speaks to the original and well-meaning concerns of compensatory justice and diversity. The problems with percentage plans lie in their effect. Overall, the existing plans have managed to admit roughly the same number of minority students as racial preference did, although Hispanics in some locations have fared better while blacks have fared worse. And reliance on geography as an equalizer points to more of those minority students being economically disadvantaged than under racial preference where many come from more affluent backgrounds and better high schools. The goal of opening up opportunity is being accomplished. But at what cost? Many of the minority students who are admitted will be less prepared than the ones admitted under preference. Instead of being the best among minorities in a competition that extends statewide and beyond, students need only to shine at their own high schools, no matter how weak those schools are. Minorities who attend schools that are strong academically, and who may be significantly stronger than the top students at the weaker schools, will fail to qualify under the percentage plan because they're beaten out by white and Asian students. We can expect the students with the weaker backgrounds to struggle academically. And we can expect them to face the double-edged negative psychology of feelings of inferiority on their own part and feelings of resentment from whites who remember well-prepared high-school classmates who lost out in the percentage plan. Colleges today face the dilemma of what to do with more students with weaker backgrounds – let them flounder in a sink-or-swim environment, or pour scarce resources into expanding remedial programs for them. The percentage-plan approach adds to the difficulty.

Beyond higher education, the percentage plans can impact high schools and society in general. They reinforce racial segregation by being a disincentive for minority families to integrate white neighborhoods and to attend better high schools. The plans remove a reason for students to strive for the true top and reach the achievement level of the larger arena beyond their own schools. And they make it easy for weak schools to avoid improvement, since their graduates can gain admission to their state's top public colleges anyway. When the measure of success is restricted to local terms, much stands to be lost. It lowers the bar rather than pushing education ahead through competition from the outside as an incentive.

The key to percentage plans is that they look beyond the factor of race, although their ultimate purpose traces to race. And in particular they encompass students from economically disadvantaged areas and schools. Another proposed substitute for racial preference that follows the economic lead even further is to aim preference directly at low-income students. For some of its proponents this is another back-door means for enrolling minorities, based on the fact that many black and Hispanic students come from low-income backgrounds. Other proponents see it as more enlightened than racial preference, believing that disadvantaged students deserve compensatory justice but that true disadvantage lies in economic circumstances rather than, or more than, skin color or ethnicity. In any event, the purpose is to help the underdog. As with percentage plans, while the extent to which it's meant as a subterfuge opens a question about legitimacy, the overall purpose of helping people who are disadvantaged to better themselves reaches moral high ground. And like percentage plans and affirmative action, the difficulty comes with putting purpose into practice.

A major obstacle many colleges face in admitting more low-income students is funding. For those students to enroll, they need financial aid, and to attract them to high-cost schools, much of it needs to be in the form of grants rather than loans. Bankrolling a mandate to give preference to economically disadvantaged students constitutes a large expense. Some of the wealthiest schools have committed to the expense, and they now allow needy students to attend for free. Most colleges can't afford it. But for the ones that can, and the others if they could, how is it to be determined just which students are economically disadvantaged? It's one thing to define disadvantage for the purpose of deciding how much financial aid to award, but another thing to define it as a reason for preference in admission. For financial aid, a sliding scale can be applied to award varying amounts of money for varying degrees of need. That approach doesn't fit in admissions, where the decision is a zero-sum pronouncement – a student is admitted or isn't. Does an applicant whose family earns a few dollars less than another applicant's family get preference while the other one doesn't? How can it be taken into account that economic status runs along a continuum, and differences among people can be vague and confusing? Any cutoff is arbitrary. Add here the problem of creative accounting as people fill out financial aid forms when the full force of admission or rejection is on the line. That temptation will be great. And then consider changes in a student's status over time – the minority status affirmative action is based on comes with birth and doesn't change, but income status can change dramatically.

And beyond income, what about the rest of the story? If we truly want to determine how disadvantaged a student's life has been, simply using income as a proxy can be misleading. Some low-income students attend relatively good schools. Will a "strength of school" factor be added to the factor of income? Will being raised in a two-parent home, having access to a computer, or any of various other advantages be taken into account that complicate a determination of just who has and who hasn't led a life lacking in opportunity?

Colleges, of course, can take these factors into account if they want to commit admissions-office resources to doing that. But if in fact they do, and they identify those students whose lives have been overwhelmingly "up against it," and if they not only admit those students but also provide funding for them, will the purpose of low-income preference be accomplished? Those proponents who favor it as a way to admit minorities will be frustrated when minority students lose out to the many disadvantaged white and Asian students they'll have to compete with. Black and Hispanic students don't have a corner on poverty or on other factors that contribute to being disadvantaged.

Regardless of their race, though, students admitted under economic preference will all face the obstacle of underpreparedness. Those who are not minorities will still encounter a negative mindset – not about race but about economic status – with feelings of inferiority and victimization, and when the new form of preference becomes known, they'll confront a reduced incentive to achieve. In many cases they won't be suspected by their peers to be preference admits, but given the baggage they'll carry in their minds added to the fact that they start out behind other students, there is a danger that underpreparedness will lead to underperformance, which will lead to needing preference again for admission to graduate school, and so on.

Instead of creating a mismatch like this, what can wealthy colleges with enough money to support economically disadvantaged students do that would truly be in the students' best interest? It's tempting to say that for the ones who are close to meeting admissions standards, give them a try, and justify that by reasoning that they're familiar with struggle and can overcome obstacles. Perhaps this will work for some, but a more comprehensive answer for all is to help them to locate a different school, one where they fit in well academically (where they qualify without preference), and provide them with the financial aid they need to attend. Perhaps that school is another college, and perhaps it's a prep school where a fifth year at the secondary level will prepare them for entry into college at a more selective level than they're ready for yet. Colleges are unlikely to offer this generosity, of course, but the suggestion makes the point that giving preference to economically disadvantaged students is not what's best for those students. What's best for them is to be matched with colleges where they fit comfortably into the academic profile.

In Sum

Minority preference in college admissions grew out of the noble purpose of making up for what minority students lacked due to their historical conditions, and of bringing them up to par with the rest of society. That purpose still exists in sentiment, but today the call is for diversity – putting students of varied racial and ethnic backgrounds together so they'll understand one another and prepare for life in a multicultural setting. Unfortunately, the program designed to accomplish these purposes hasn't worked. Minority students still lag as far behind in standardized measures of academic accomplishment as they did when affirmative action began. Supporters argue that preference has been successful anyway by putting more minorities into the professions, but that thinking rests on the faulty assumption that they needed to attend prestigious colleges to do so. It's also claimed that having a diverse population of students on campus will allow them to mix with one another, yet colleges are full of separatism in the curriculum through ethnic studies programs and in student life through segregated living arrangements and social programs. The preference minority students receive is a cause of resentment among whites and Asians as well as a source of anxiety for minorities themselves. Rather than leading the way as we strive for a just society with the races living in harmony, affirmative action has become an entrenched entitlement with no end in sight. The implicit and noxious message is that minorities have lesser capability that the rest of society should make accommodation for. This isn't the original purpose of affirmative action, but it looms as an unfortunate legacy. We're caught in a version of the "white man's burden" in which virtue goes in and condescension comes out. The ugly irony is that a means designed to combat racism in our society instead perpetuates it.

Alternative approaches meant to disguise or replace minority preference also run into problems. Percentage plans draw minority students, but with the need for even more remedial help than under affirmative action. The strategy for this approach can work only in states heavy with de facto segregated schools, and it results in minority students from weak high schools being winners while stronger minority students from stronger schools lose out. A system of preference based on economic status is one more way of bringing in academically marginal students who are likely to struggle. It may frustrate minority advocates by selecting many disadvantaged whites and Asians, and confuse everyone involved since just what constitutes disadvantage is often variable and vague.

Instead of rationalizing the worth of affirmative action, or stretching to find alternatives, what's needed is to recognize the educational and social distortions that have grown out of good intentions. A simpler course of action is due. Minority preference should be eliminated. For minority students to have true opportunity and respect, they should be treated as equals and expected to perform as equals. Anything else is a vote of no confidence – an expectation of lesser performance and an insinuation of lesser capability.

– 4 –

LEGACIES, FINANCE, AND FAIRNESS

The raging debate of recent years over minority preference in college admissions has raised the visibility of another type of preference that's a regular part of the competition to get into selective schools – for the relatives of alumni. It's no secret that legacies are admitted at a much higher rate to our nation's top colleges than applicants in general, and with affirmative action under fire, what's been called "affirmative action for the rich" has drawn shots as well.

Supporters of minority preference see hypocrisy and injustice in giving favoritism to a group known to be white and affluent without giving it also to those who are non-white and largely from the other end of the economic spectrum. The simple logic behind this view is based on the American penchant for fairness – a disdain for aristocracy and plutocracy, and a belief in giving equal opportunity. While there is a strong point to be recognized here, it shouldn't be taken as a single or final answer about legacies. The reasons colleges have for giving them preference are far from the reasons for minority preference, and each type of preference should be evaluated on its own terms. This isn't to lose sight of a concern for justice, but to realize that other factors should be taken into account and carefully considered.

Looking into American history, we find that legacy preference as we know it today didn't exist until the 20th century. Prior to that time only a tiny portion of the population attended college. Even at well-known institutions, students who had money to pay for tuition found their way in if they had the necessary academic background. Successive generations of a family attending the same college would have been appreciated by the administration, but wasn't then the influential factor it proved to be later when admittance became competitive. During the 20th century several factors caused competition to arise, and eventually grow to the high-intensity level we have today. An increasing percentage of people wanted postsecondary schooling, and families that in the past had counted on easy entry for their children to their prestigious alma maters found that up-and-comers from various sectors were crowding the field. Early on there was a concern about a disproportionately large number of Jews. Later in the century there was a similar concern about Asians. Along the way most single-sex colleges became coed, and the civil rights movement opened the way for black and Hispanic students. The applicant pool at the most desired schools grew continuously. Colleges looked for ways to hold on to their roots and provide admission for alumni children, and at the same time reward high achievement and increase diversity. Legacy policies were adopted gradually as institutions individually reached their pressure points. Today at the most selective ones, competition has heightened to the extent that one in five to fewer than one in ten applicants is accepted. Nearly all of these schools give legacy preference, and legacies account for perhaps one in seven students in the freshman class (between 10 percent and 25 percent depending on the school). As the selectivity scale descends, the importance of legacy preference does also, but even at institutions with moderate selectivity, it's often a factor. A comprehensive accounting of how many applicants are affected, and to what degree, is hard to come by because college officials reveal as little as possible about the legacy system. They're well aware of its general unpopularity – 75 percent of the public opposes it, according to polling data.

In spite of a strong disapproval rating, and the offense it gives to the American sense of fairness, legacy preference remains firmly in place. College officials are uncomfortable when they're challenged to justify it, but they have an established rationale for why favoritism toward alumni is not only acceptable, but an important feature in the way they operate. When critics ask indignantly, why, in the face of democratic ideals, access to the highly sought precious commodity colleges hold is made easier for some people because of who their parents are, the response comes in three main arguments. We're told that admissions decisions are the result of a holistic process. Beyond academics, legacy is only one of several factors considered, along with preference for minorities, for students with special talents like athletics or music, for first-generation college students, and for those from remote geographical locations. It's often said that within this complicated mix, the bump given to legacies is merely a tie-breaker among similarly qualified applicants. After all, while many legacies get acceptances, many others don't. Legacy preference is described in terms of "other things being equal." In other words, the preference given is minimal.

A second argument embraces a respect for family. Alumni of a college are the institution's extended family. They do volunteer work for it and talk it up in enthusiastic terms. They assist in recruiting and fundraising. They show a loyalty that other people don't. Their sons and daughters grow up hearing stories about the school and may have made visits to the campus. They arrive as freshmen already feeling a special connection to their college, and with a special incentive to represent their bloodline well. Legacies and their parents offer an intangible quality that is uniquely theirs. Colleges want it and are willing to give preference for it, all the while preserving family ties.

Third, what colleges count on even more from their family affair is something quite tangible – money. Alumni give donations to their alma maters, sometimes large ones, that are counted on for the general budget, some of which ends up as financial aid for needy students. Officials point out that if they don't hold up their end of the arrangement by giving preference for legacies, alumni will give less money, and the quality of the services the schools offers will suffer. And they'll be less able to make a top-flight education available to students from low-income families. Here is the argument legacy proponents rely on when the other arguments prove unconvincing. Social utility directs us to accept a practice that strains moral sensibility on the one hand, but on the other hand accomplishes an obvious good. This is the trade-off colleges are willing to make, and which they find justified in practical terms.

The holistic admissions argument is based on an analogy – legacy preference is like several other kinds of preference, each of which identifies students by a certain characteristic they possess that colleges desire. If it's fair to give preference for the other characteristics, then it's fair to give it for legacy status. The problem with this line of thinking is that being a legacy is not like having the other characteristics, but in fact is quite different. Legacy preference is drawn entirely from the status of students' ancestors rather than from a quality they possess on their own. Preference based on a talent – athletics, music, debate, acting, and others – is for something that resides in the students themselves. It's presence on campus strengthens the student body by making it well-rounded. A related claim is made for minority preference – the characteristic in question isn't a talent, but the students themselves are counted on to round out the mix and enhance the learning experience for others. All of these forms of preference aim at diversity of one sort or another, and all bring recognizable contributions that students make with their presence. The factor of legacy status alone imparts no special something that is meant to enhance the student body. So the analogy breaks down. It doesn't work to claim that it's fair to give legacy preference if it's fair to give the other preferences colleges have designated.

Sometimes alongside the holistic approach, we hear the claim that the advantage legacies get amounts to no more than a tie-breaker. Not only is legacy merely a single factor among several in a complicated mix, but it's downplayed further by suggesting the weight it carries is slight. Not all colleges make this claim, but when they do, critics are suspicious that they're hearing wishful thinking more than reality. Statistics suggest the critics are right. One study of three elite schools determined the advantage for legacies, with "other things equal," to be worth 160 points of SAT score. Another study of 30 highly selective institutions found that the sons and daughters of alumni hold a 45 percent edge over other applicants. College officials may counter that what characterizes a few schools hasn't been proven for the rest, but this is a feeble defense without data to back it up. Still, what if it could be shown that the break legacies get, at least in many cases, is not conspicuously large and is more like a slight bump? Would that deflate the charge that legacy preference is unfair to other applicants? When a bump is among equals, it may seem minimal, but in the zero-sum atmosphere of college admissions, it really is much more. At a school where only a small percentage of the applicants will be admitted, and a large percentage of them are well qualified and roughly equal, a bump is crucial. It creates the needed separation to be chosen. In a closely contested race, the difference between the one taking the prize and the rest of the pack may be small. But one goes home a winner and the rest do not.

Still another twist in holistic thinking is to tackle the core notions of fairness and merit that are generally believed to shape the selection process. Admissions officials say the process they follow doesn't submit to fairness. They wish the public would understand that. Their job is to craft a well-rounded class, one that balances various characteristics colleges want on their campuses. They create a blend in which students can learn from one another because of the contribution each one makes to the whole. Rather than trying to be fair, admissions is directed by a sense of proportion. Admissions decisions are an art, and in the creativity of art, fairness has no meaning.

Fairness goes hand-in-hand with merit. People expect that when colleges rate applicants, they'll do it based on meritorious performance – demonstrated accomplishment as found in grades and test scores in particular, and sometimes special talents. When they see applicants with lesser credentials selected ahead of others with greater ones, they cry foul. But this assumption, we learn, is confused. Merit conceived in this way is a misnomer. A revised understanding of merit sees it as more than academics and performance, and as extending more broadly to other characteristics or conditions students bring to campus that can benefit the school. This point is sometimes used to support minority preference, and it's applied to legacy preference as well. When the admissions process is disparaged for failing to make judgments based on merit, the reason is that "merit" has been too narrowly defined.

These appeals labor hard to stretch common sense and common usage. Extending beyond grades and test scores may be helpful in putting together a well rounded-class – to get a varied but balanced group that find one another interesting, and are able to learn from one another and appreciate one another's talents. But even if the conventional notion of fairness is turned aside in this way by a push for diversity, that doesn't make room for legacy preference. Because legacies add nothing to the student pool, renouncing an intention of fairness, no matter how enlightened that maneuver may seem, provides no justification for giving them preference. As for the revised meaning of merit, it defies both the dictionary and everyday speech. Merit, according to language experts, is an excellence or virtue. It refers to having a superior quality, a demonstrated ability or achievement. When the term is applied to specifics, we hear of merit pay, merit badge, merit scholarship, all implying a praiseworthy activity has been performed that justifies a reward. Legacies simply don't fit here, nor do minorities. To be a legacy isn't to have achieved anything. There is no excellence involved. It occurs simply as an accident of birth, and to give preference to people on that basis hits a nerve in a society with a long tradition of respecting hard work and accomplishment.

The perspective on fairness and merit emerging from the admissions establishment has the ring of postmodern thinking that is common philosophical fare in higher education – transcending morality and reinventing language. But intellectualizing the situation in this way will come off as avant-garde to the general public, including applicants and their parents, who are looking for a straightforward message. It doesn't excuse the mistaken logic of including legacy among a group of preferences meant to diversify the student body, and it doesn't excuse the misleading claim that the advantage legacies get is minimal. Asking people to accept the holistic rationale for legacy admissions is asking them to bend their common sense.

When advocates for the legacy system feel pressed to go beyond an appeal to holism, they sometimes turn to the "we are family" explanation. With a good speaker giving it an eloquent presentation, it can sound warm and friendly, and in tune with respected values. Being part of a family is a desirable thing, and the give and take involved is understandable. A family takes care of its own, the members do things for one another that other people don't, providing a cohesiveness and continuity. When favoritism for alumni and their children is associated with a cherished unit of society, it comes off as acceptable, perhaps even admirable. Once the affectionate prose is peeled back, however, the argument that's exposed is rather ordinary, and very thin.

The give and take of "family" is a transaction. In return for preference in admission, the members going to college are counted on to feel at home immediately when they set foot on campus, and to have the special incentive of doing well to uphold their family tie. So there is a quality, after all, legacies can be said to have that benefits their school. Unfortunately, while loyalty and enthusiasm are factors colleges desire, they don't warrant the reward of admissions preference. Is the good feeling legacies have for their college any more valuable than the gratitude and pride other applicants who are accepted will have? Might legacies take their position for granted and be less favorably inclined toward their school than someone who was admitted knowing the decision was based purely on demonstrated ability? In any event, it isn't necessary to give legacy preference in order to have upbeat students. School spirit isn't something unique to the children of alumni or that can be assumed to be in greater abundance with them. In fact, it might be asked if it would be as evident as with other students. Their family status is something legacies generally aren't eager to have talked about on campus, since they'd be suspected of lacking the credentials to get in without it.

What about parents? Their contribution to their college family is problematic, too, although the claim at least is for services rendered, while for students it rests merely on an attitude. Alumni are heralded as recruiters. But how much recruiting help do the schools where legacy status is most valued actually need, when they have several to ten or more applicants for every seat in the freshman class? And how much help can alumni give? A few of them make calls to parents of students the admissions office has accepted, to try to seal the deal. And some schools have them conduct off-campus interviews of applicants. But only a tiny percentage of alumni do this. More people are counted on to talk up their schools casually with friends and acquaintances. But a realistic expectation of the result is minimal. Colleges' reputations today are carried through the mass media. Pronouncements by *U.S. News* and other national publications hold the power. Guidance counselors exercise some sway in venturing their professional opinions, but they're frustrated by the overwhelming influence the major publications have. In comparison, word of mouth from alumni pales. However enthusiastic, it tends to be anecdotal. However well meaning, it's not the word of an expert. And it reaches a very limited number of people.

Fundraising is the other "family" duty alumni are supposed to perform, both influencing other people to give and giving themselves. In terms of influence, they may host dinners or receptions, and use corporate contacts to ask for gifts. Here is a clear benefit they provide. But again, only a very few do these things. And when they do, how much money do they raise? How much do they raise that wouldn't or couldn't be raised without them? And, if they have no expectation of legacy preference, will they still give their services to the alumni family? These questions are difficult to answer, but they suggest the benefit colleges gain from alumni acting as fundraisers may be limited in the grand scheme of things and lack the sort of necessity needed to make a reasonable claim that admissions preference is warranted in return.

Still, it isn't the role of alumni as fundraising intermediaries that colleges are most interested in. The greatest desire is for them to make donations on their own. This is the chief reason legacy preference continues to exist in spite of concerns about its fairness. The main argument for treating alumni children as a favored group in admissions is that it inspires financial contributions from their parents that wouldn't be made otherwise. Alumni give money, and they expect something in particular in return. If they can't count on it, they won't give, or they'll give less. When the argument is cast in monetary terms like this, the concept of the college "family" harmonizing as a social unit is put aside. Realpolitik takes over. There is a tacit recognition that without the social utility claimed to result from legacy preference, the practice would be on shaky ground. The point is that an amount of basic fairness is given up in order to achieve a recognized good. This point plays out not only in moral terms but legal terms as well.

Unlike minority preference, which is tracked through landmark Supreme Court cases, the legality of legacy preference is largely untested, although it draws attention when affirmative action is criticized. General opinion is that the practice is acceptable, with conventional thinking using the same reasoning that cleared the legal path to boost minority admissions – giving preference to a certain group results in a demonstrable benefit for colleges and for society as a whole. The benefit attributed to minorities is that their presence on campus broadens all students' perspectives, and better prepares them for life in a multicultural society. The benefit drawn from legacies is that the money their parents donate is instrumental for ensuring a good quality education is available for all, and for providing college-based financial aid for needy students. While the benefits for the two types of preference are very different from one another, the assumption is that they're both covered by the same umbrella.

This line of thinking may soon face a legal challenge. The highest-level decision on record about legacy preference was at the state level and occurred in 1976. It did find the argument about alumni financial contributions to be permissible constitutionally, but that was only one among other challenges dealt with in a case about preference for state residents applying to a public college. Little detail was offered about legacies, and preference for them was separated from minority preference, which was accepted on the justification (that today is legally untenable) of making up for racial inequality. Recently two new arguments have been presented by legal scholars to assert that legacy preference is, in fact, unlawful.

One line of thinking appeals to the often forgotten Nobility Clause of the Constitution, which says that state governments cannot grant titles of nobility, such as duke or earl, that recognize privilege based on lineage. The argument is that what the Founders meant isn't merely the naming of individuals, but government-sponsored hereditary privilege in general, which should apply to the practice of giving legacy privilege in college admissions at state-sponsored institutions. Proponents of this approach note that if attempts were made today to give an advantage to public-sector applicants elsewhere, other than to colleges, they would be considered flagrantly unacceptable – for instance, adding points on civil service exams for the children of state employees. Thought of in this way, legacy privilege is historically out of step, a contemporary vestige of the practice of giving government-endorsed perks for family status, something the very founding of our nation rejected.

Another argument that looks to the Constitution cites the Equal Protection clause of the 14th Amendment. The amendment was installed in 1868 to support fair treatment for blacks, but its wording was more general than that, and its purpose has been established as being wider. This point has been stated directly in legal opinions by the Supreme Court, and the court has applied the equal protection principle in deciding a variety of cases against discrimination not only for race but for ancestry in other ways and parents' marital status. By extension, it applies to legacy status as well, which is a prime example of unequal treatment based on differences in ancestry. As with the Nobility Clause, the 14th Amendment deals with rights conferred by the powers of the states, so it applies to public institutions. The argument doesn't cover private colleges. A related strategy, though, based on a different law, does. The Civil Rights Act of 1866, which was inspired by the same thinking as the 14th Amendment, prohibits discrimination based on race and, more broadly, ancestry. Two late-20th-century Supreme Court cases found the law to apply to private schools, but those cases didn't specifically test legacy admissions at colleges. Here is a possible means to target both private and public colleges for discrimination based on ancestry.

Whether these arguments take root, or instead are shrugged off as out of date or eccentric, remains to be seen. While they haven't provoked a court case as yet, the lack of legal decisions on record invites a test and encourages new thinking. But regardless of the legal standing of legacy preference, the claim colleges make that it's crucial for fundraising runs into other problems. What seems like a sensible proposition – that special treatment in admissions for alumni is needed to secure a crucial source of financing that will do social good – turns out to be dubious when it's examined. One main problem is a lack of statistical data to support it. The claim is nearly always presented as an article of faith, and if colleges have done self-studies to back it up, they've seldom reported them to the public. However, one elite school that released information about a major fundraising campaign for one year (2006) reported that 65 percent of legacy parents contributed an average of $34,000 each, while donors without a legacy child were at 40 percent and $4,000. These numbers back up the perception that the legacy connection brings in strong donations, although it may be suspected that the $34,000 average was skewed by one or several very large contributions. A more complicated study of another single school traced a longitudinal pattern of alumni giving over 20 years ending in 2006. It found that alumni with children were slightly more likely to contribute than those without children, and that contributions for families with children who applied to the school increased about 20 percent during the teen years before the applications were made. Again we find support, if only mild, for the fundraising claim, but the devil comes out in the further details.

The same study showed that when legacies were rejected, their parents stopped giving, although how long the holdout continued is unclear. For accepted students, the elevated family contributions continued for only three or four years and then went back to the level for alumni with young children. It was also revealed that 70 percent of the total amount of alumni contributions came from the top 1 percent of gifts, leaving only 30 percent of the money coming from the rank-and-file 99 percent of donors. A further reading of the data concluded that half of the giving by alumni with children derived from altruism and only half from the hoped-for gain in the admissions process. With this information, the apparent financial gain from offering preference to legacies begins to erode.

Further questions can be raised that weaken the case even more. Assuming that alumni parents of spurned applicants stop giving for at least a few years, doesn't that loss offset their heavier than normal giving in the prior years? What will the giving pattern of alumni parents be like if legacy preference doesn't exist? If they know in advance there is no alumni-connected advantage in admissions, will they fail to give or to give as much? Or will they simply give for other reasons, and without clustering their giving around the high-school and college years of their children? And what if alumni do decide not to give to their alma maters because their children won't be going there (the worst-case scenario supporters of the legacy system fear)? They may instead give to the colleges their children attend, still putting money into higher education. When a school loses out on a donation because an alumni son or daughter is rejected or doesn't apply, it may make up for it in a donation from the parents of a nonlegacy who got the admissions spot the legacy didn't get.

With these questions and complicating factors undermining the worth claimed for legacy preference in fundraising, should we assume there is such a worth at all? A recent study says no. A detailed analysis of the period 1998 through 2008, drawing from data banks higher education institutions report to, covered the top 100 national universities in the *U.S. News* rankings. The conclusion was that no causal relationship exists between legacy preference and total alumni giving – favoritism for legacies in the admissions process doesn't increase the amount of money donated by an institution's graduates. Schools with legacy preference do have higher alumni giving than schools without it, the study found, but that's because the students they admit are wealthier than their peers at non-legacy schools. The determining factor in how much alumni give is how well-heeled they are, not that they're enticed by the prospect of securing admission for their sons and daughters. This leads to a question about whether dropping legacy preference, which a few schools have done in recent years, may lead to a financial loss – since replacing legacy admits with other admits means replacing students from wealthier families with students from less wealthy families. The study found that in the short term that's not the case, and if an impact is to be felt, it will take at least a generation. What accounts for the lack of harm may be another factor the researchers found about the relative importance of alumni giving in the grand scheme of an institution's budget. At half of the schools in the study, it was 3.5 percent – or less – of total expenditures. The more analysis that is done about the supposed financial benefit colleges derive from legacy preference, the less that benefit appears to be, if it exists at all.

Without the fundraising gain legacy preference is supposed to create, the social utility justification that's claimed to support it disappears. The gist of the claim is that giving up an amount of admissions fairness to make a substantial financial gain is an acceptable trade-off. But if the financial gain is dubious – negligible or nonexistent – fairness is given away for no reason. Unless or until colleges provide detailed data to prove there is a financial advantage connected to legacy preference, the enlarged social good they claim to be achieving is a myth. But what if the data were available, and it showed that favoring alumni in admissions does yield a clear monetary advantage for colleges? Even then, the social utility that resulted would be problematic. Based on a principle of gain outweighing loss, it should attempt to maximize the former and minimize the latter. The legacy preference system doesn't do that. It gives preference to a large group of people when only some of them will provide more than trifling financial support, and a tiny number may account for the bulk of it. Critics have suggested that as much or more money could be raised by selling a small number of seats in the freshman class at high prices. A greater utility would result, with the unfairness doled out being minimized to a few cases. A much greater efficiency would be achieved. Admissions could eliminate legacy preference but retain the fundraising advantage it's supposed to give.

While this idea may seem unacceptably venal, it serves as a reminder about the shaky moral standing of the practice it would replace. And the replacement itself is nothing new in higher education. An even more objectionable category of finance-related admissions preference than legacies, and one colleges are even less comfortable talking about, carries the euphemistic label "development case." The sons and daughters of hefty donors can expect a hefty boost in the admissions process. The preference colleges now offer to large numbers of legacies in exchange for financial gain could be replaced by taking in a few more development admits, with the financial picture remaining unchanged.

Whether it's selling seats openly, doing it quietly through development cases, or engaging in the related practice of legacy preference, colleges are striking a bargain that many people see as wrong – wrong per se, not just in a qualified sense. Even if the bargain is profitable, it bumps up against basic fairness. The financial argument for legacy preference is based in utilitarian thinking, and a major weakness in utilitarianism is that it doesn't account for fundamental moral principles that refuse to be compromised even by large sums of money or other inducements. What is the right price for giving up equal opportunity? Or to put it another way, can financial gain couched in terms of social utility ever make up for the erosion it causes in the just society that our colleges profess to be striving for? College officials need to be asking themselves just what amount of utility, if any amount, is sufficient in return for a practice that is highly divisive.

When confronted on these terms, supporters of legacy preference sometimes appeal to a different but equally fundamental principle in our society – freedom of association. This freedom wasn't written into the Constitution explicitly, but is regarded as a derivative of the First Amendment guarantees of speech and assembly. Private institutions generally have the right to determine the kinds of people they will associate with, although certain exceptions have been found by the courts in the past several decades. When the right is applied to higher education, it's taken to mean that while public colleges have obligations to the overall population, and the propriety of legacy admission at those schools is debatable, private schools have the right to admit whomever they want.

This explanation runs into trouble when we ask about the true nature of private colleges. Just how private are they? They promote themselves to the general public as being available to that public, in order to draw as many applicants as possible. And they serve the public purpose of training future leaders for the whole of society. Most importantly, they receive public funding, especially from the federal government. Large amounts of it are dispensed to research programs, and besides this, much of the tuition students pay comes from financial aid drawn from federal sources. With a strong public connection like this, leaning on freedom of association for support opens the legacy system to a possible challenge from Washington. There are two approaches that could be taken, one involving the Internal Revenue Service. When colleges claim that preference for alumni children is needed for fundraising, they risk running up against the federal tax code, which exempts both donors and recipients from paying taxes on charitable deductions. The write-off is premised on the idea that no personal benefit flows from recipient to donor. The giver is not to be enriched, the motive for giving should be altruism. If it's established in legal terms that there is an expected quid pro quo in donations – something colleges now claim as the main reason for giving legacy preference, and that they'll be forced to demonstrate clearly if they're taken to court on a charge of discrimination as may happen with the new legal strategies mentioned earlier – then the tax code is being violated. Both alumni parents and their alma maters would be ineligible for the deductions they now get, at least for the amount of the quid pro quo involved between donor and donee. Colleges are caught in a dilemma. They can admit that legacy preference gives them financial gain, and risk losing a tax deduction. Or they can maintain that it doesn't bring financial gain, and jeopardize a foundation piece they need for a defense of legacy preference in court against a charge of discrimination.

Beyond targeting tax deductions, the other means for federal government action against legacy preference is for Congress to recognize the practice as discriminatory and to inform colleges that if they continue with it they're subject to a loss of federal funding. Doing this would draw cries from colleges' leaders that the government is issuing heavy-handed controls, but the protest would be at the expense of drawing attention to a special privilege a large majority of the public opposes. Whether Congress could bring itself to take this action is unknown. And whether colleges would give in rather than fight against it is unknown as well. But a precedent already exists with another issue of access to institutions of higher education – regarding the right of military recruiters to visit campuses when some schools had banned them because they disapproved of the military's regulations about homosexuality. The threat of withholding funds was the leverage that brought dissenting colleges into compliance. Congress's power to do that was challenged in the courts and upheld by the U. S. Supreme Court in 2006 in a unanimous decision that said colleges had overinterpreted the freedom given them by the First Amendment.

Legacy preference is ripe for a legal battle. The assumptions colleges make that they stand on safe ground constitutionally – that they're not susceptible to having Equal Protection or other clauses applied against them, and that they're shielded by freedom of association – are questionable and may encounter tough going. Colleges should take note. But they shouldn't need Congressional action or court cases to force them to stop a practice that advantages a subset of applicants who offer no special quality to add to the student body. The moral arena is where the future of legacy preference should be decided, and there it's a losing proposition. If the leaders of our top higher education institutions find themselves clinging to a questionable legal claim to justify their support for hereditary privilege, they should realize they're off the mark. Instead of taking the position that "If we can get away with it legally, we will," they should vow to "do the right thing." None of the justifications that are offered for legacy preference work. The right thing is to admit this and get rid of a nasty blight that afflicts college admissions.

– 5 –

BIG-TIME
"AMATEUR" SPORTS

Big-time college sports enjoy great popularity – with the players who participate and the many others who dream of it, with the millions of fans who watch the spectacles in person and on TV, and with college officials who like the media exposure and revenue they generate. But there is a controversial side as well. Many people within academia as well as outside of it denounce what major college athletic programs do as compromising the academic mission of higher education. Especially, there are two main points the critics make. One is that big-time sports are not conducted at the amateur level and are professional except in name. The other point is that professionalized sports run counter to higher education's purpose, that the benefits they bring to colleges are offset by the harm they cause.

The leadership of the college sports establishment – the schools' presidents and athletic directors along with officials of the National Collegiate Athletic Association – pay lip service to the criticism and remain committed to the status quo. Their response consists of a defense mechanism of tired arguments supplemented by occasional tinkering with the established rules. The elephant in the back yard is made to shift its feet, while its handlers swear it really does belong there. What's needed is an admission that the elephant just doesn't fit, that the troubling conditions do truly require being fixed. A major change is a must.

But what should the change consist of? While the critics are right about the problems they find, devising a fix to the situation is no easy matter. Sports enthusiasts fear the formula will be to eliminate or downsize the present structure. Doing this would not only answer the problems, but also leave a large and distressing void, since, as their opponents point out, it would decimate a popular form of public entertainment and a way of life desired by young people with certain skills. And colleges would lose a public relations tool and a cherished rallying point for school spirit. Here is the impasse that needs to be overcome for change to reach a proper end. The righteous cause should understand the collateral damage it can do to an established social institution, and seek a fair and reasonable course of action. That course is available – if defenders of the present system are willing to admit that what they're engaged in is professional athletics, and to accept a restructuring that, although radical, maintains big-time teams while getting back on track toward academic integrity.

THE PICTURE WE SEE – AMATEUR OR PROFESSIONAL?

College sports are now a multibillion dollar per year enterprise. While some of that amount is accounted for by the many colleges that field small-time teams on modest budgets, most of it traces to the big-time programs where the top ones work with budgets of $100 million, and individual teams are slated for a few million to $50 million or more. It's no surprise to find the big-time teams behaving like businesses. The overall pattern is tied closely to making money and spending money, with an eye on catering to fans.

- *TV contracts* between networks and college sports leagues have long been a part of the college sports scene. A more recent move is for leagues and individual schools to establish their own networks. These ventures aim for a larger share of the sports dollars generated through television and look for ways to promote sports like gymnastics, volleyball, track and field, and others in addition to the standard fare of football and basketball.
- *Corporate sponsorships* provide substantial income for athletic departments. Deals with clothing and shoe companies, and for signage, naming rights for stadiums and buildings, and royalties from licensing school logos run well into the millions of dollars per year per school.
- *Appearance fees* for football can reach from half a million to a million dollars per game for the most sought-after schools. Weak teams are paid to play, and almost surely lose, against powerhouse teams at the powerhouses' home sites, and without requiring a return game at their own home sites.
- *Coaches' contracts* in football and basketball are regularly hitting the million-dollar-per-year figure, with some at two, three, or four million, and escalation ever apparent. The numbers often rival those of major-league pro coaches and exceed those of minor-league pros. Coaches move easily back and forth between college teams and professional teams.
- *Players are paid*, through tuition wavers and living expenses, to play for their teams. They're required to follow rigorous practice schedules, and for many, the total time

they put into their sports is the equivalent of a full-time job (despite NCAA regulations against it).

- The *stadiums and arenas* teams play in are often as large as those of major-league professional teams, and upgrades now have schools installing luxury features such as skyboxes. Attendance at games often equals that of the pros.
- *Leagues* form, and teams join or drop out of them, according to the opportunities to maximize profits for the teams. Some leagues easily cover more geographical territory than professional minor leagues.
- The *NCAA*, the organization responsible for ensuring that players are student-athletes who are getting an education, also functions as the chief agent for college sports in general by sponsoring national tournaments, brokering deals with TV networks, and sharing in the profits.
- Super fans, aka *boosters*, have a significant involvement in the finances of certain college teams, making large donations in return for premium seating, a place in the team's entourage, and influence (often not admitted) in administrative affairs.

The picture we see in big-time college sports bears these marks of a commercial enterprise. It shows little resemblance to the pastime we associate traditionally with the ideal of amateurism – where the emphasis is on the well-being of the participants and activity pursued for its own sake. Yet college officials refuse to acknowledge that their major sports teams are professional. They cling to the amateur label because it allows them to continue operating comfortably as nonprofit organizations – they're shielded from the considerable financial impact they would face if it were acknowledged they were running taxable businesses. What they're saying, essentially, is that participation in college sports is part of the educational mission of their institutions, and that whatever money is made from sports is only incidental.

The key to claiming amateur status lies in the purpose of the activity in question. The dual purposes of professional sports are to provide entertainment for the public and a profit for the teams' owners. Amateur sports, on the other hand, exist for the purpose of enhancing the educational experience of the athletes. Besides simply having fun and finding an outlet for their physical energy, they acquire practical lessons about life. Through the extracurriculum they develop virtues such as responsibility, self-discipline and self-sacrifice, time management, commitment to excellence, and leadership. The apologists for big-time sports steadfastly maintain that imparting these virtues is what the public extravaganzas the athletes participate in is all about. The entertainment value and huge sums of money involved just happen to accompany the opportunity being offered to athletes to learn their extracurricular lessons about life.

To claim that amateurism is the true purpose of contests that often draw crowds larger than those watching major league pro teams is merely a pretense, one that might be accepted with a wink but not in seriousness. When large numbers of spectators and large amounts of money are involved, the ideal of amateurism gives way to professionalism. Common sense says as much. Large crowds and big-time financing aren't necessary to accomplish the objectives of amateurism. Student-athletes can learn their value lessons playing before a crowd of any size, for teams that have modest budgets, and where admission is free. If colleges were not playing for the purpose of profit or entertainment, they wouldn't need the elaborate apparatus of big-time sports.

What's more, if the aim of varsity sports was to provide a learning opportunity, then surely that opportunity would be offered to as many students as possible. The schools claiming their large athletics budgets are really for the purpose of amateurism would be spending their money to field many more varsity teams. They would operate them in more sports, and would field junior varsity and freshman teams as they used to do before those teams were abolished a few decades ago so the money from them could be shifted to the varsity. Further yet, schools could have more than one varsity (or junior varsity or freshman) team per sport. A large campus, perhaps of 25,000 students or more, will have enough serious and skilled athletes wanting to play basketball, soccer, and various other sports to fill the rosters of several small-time teams competitive enough to play against comparable teams at other schools. This is the model that would dominate the landscape if colleges with deep pockets for sports followed the purpose of amateurism. But the model of professionalism is in control in a way that disallows fulfilling the amateur ideal, and instead focuses on a small number of players and large audiences, while aiming to maximize profits.

Aware that the claim of amateurism draws ridicule and disbelief, its supporters have added a clever rhetorical maneuver to prop it up. Huge television contracts and audiences of millions, we are told, don't change the inherent educational purpose of sports. The scale and popularity of an activity doesn't alter its essential nature. Colleges are just meeting a demand, as they would with other services they offer if the demand were great. If French lectures and accounting classes were as popular as sports, they, too, would be commercialized (presumably televised and drawing large revenues), but that wouldn't change their essential nature from being educational.

This reasoning may seem plausible at first glance. But it rests on a false analogy claiming a similarity between athletics and academics. Sports programs are not comparable to college academic pursuits. When sports programs are presented before a mass audience, their educational function is lost for all but the team members – only fifteen basketball players or a hundred football players go through the experiences that will teach the value lessons about self-discipline, leadership, and so on that are claimed to be so important. The audience – the thousands to millions of people who watch the sports spectacles – simply gets entertainment. If lectures on French or accounting are presented to a mass audience, the educational function of the activity carries over to that audience. What's available to them isn't simply entertainment, but learning, and all of them can get in on it. While sports and academics are parts of the same institution, one pursuit shouldn't be mistaken for the other. The notion that big-time college sports are fundamentally about learning should be put to rest.

Still another angle supporting the claim of amateurism looks beyond the athletes' experience in the playing arena and toward their status in the classroom. Pro athletes are paid to play, not to go to school. For college athletes, we're told, the situation is reversed. They're not paid to play sports, but to be members of an academic community. They are officially labeled "student-athletes," with student coming first. The problem with this perspective is that when students receive athletic scholarships, and many if not most members of big-time teams do, they are indeed paid to play. If they stop playing their sport, they stop receiving scholarship money. And if it were not for playing their sport, they wouldn't have received the money in the first place. They're paid by the school because they are athletes and as long as they are athletes. Few of them would qualify for academic scholarships, and while without sports many would be eligible for need-based financial aid, that scenario would likely involve more money in loans than in grants. The form of financial aid they'd receive as students would be substantially different from what it is for them as athletes. Scholarship athletes are hired by their schools, and not for their performance in the classroom.

While claims about values learned on the playing field and about the financial status of student-athletes are used to associate big-time sports with amateurism, another tactic aims at distancing them from the finances associated with professionalism. When forced to acknowledge the large revenue intakes involved, defenders of the system note that many of the teams actually lose money because of their large expenses. This admission is intended to elicit sympathy and a "give 'em a break" attitude, but it ought to be seen as a danger signal. It should provoke a concern that if college teams are losing money in the marketplace of athletics, they'll be a drain on resources that otherwise could go to the primary function of higher education – which isn't sports.

A picture of financial ill-health doesn't mean the teams are not operated as businesses. The suggestion of insolvency shouldn't mask the fact that billions of dollars in revenue are generated each year by big-time sports, and most of that money is spent paying the bills for those sports. Some goes for maintaining teams in sports that have few fans and little revenue intake, and just a tiny amount goes to support the intramural and club teams that are the only part of the athletics program operated at the amateur level. The budget-breaking costs are for special equipment rooms, team travel, million-dollar coaches, recruiting, and the rest of the trappings of professional athletics that go with the big-time teams.

While pleading impoverishment is tricky, given the considerable amount of revenue coming in and lavish spending going out, colleges still have their trump card to rely on. They point out that whatever money a school's athletic teams bring in and spend falls under the umbrella of a larger organization that has nonprofit status. By definition, the school is noncommercial, and tax-exempt. But even so, there is a problem. According to tax law, the exemption applies only to money used to further the primary purpose of the institution. Money spent to support major sports teams, then, should not be tax-exempt if the sports are for entertainment. Here is why defenders of the system exaggerate at great length to identify college teams with the educational value of amateurism. If the law were applied to colleges the way it is to other nonprofit organizations, big-time sports would be liable for taxes.

This means not only having to pay income tax on their profits, but also the required amounts for each of their worker-athletes to cover social security, medicare, federal and state unemployment, and workers' compensation insurance. Further, the athletes could negotiate for salaries, and perhaps join together for collective bargaining, adding still more to the cost of labor. And to top things off, the tax deductions attached to donations to athletic programs would disappear, with the likely result that many donors would reduce their giving to college sports or quit it entirely. Treating big-time sports as the financially driven industry they are would be a costly affair for colleges.

So far the schools have managed to avoid that prospect – and get away with the myth that the entertainment they sell should be immune to taxation – because Congress and the Internal Revenue Service have been especially generous in accepting and sometimes creating excuses for looking the other way, in other words, allowing a special exemption. Some commentators have suggested that among the Congressional decision makers there are alumni and sports fans who were motivated to stand behind their favorite teams. A more favorable reading of the lawmakers' motivation sees it as a genuine desire to help higher education by ensuring that colleges have enough funding to operate their extracurricular activities. But whatever the impetus, the nonenforcement of tax laws allows the riches of big-time college sports to be treated like the proceeds from a small, local fundraiser. When a high school team or a small-time college team raises money for new uniforms the school's budget can't afford, or to send a bus to take fans to an away game, no one calls in the tax officials. The bake-sale principal applies – nobody wants to tax the bake-sale proceeds that provide a small supplement for a team. But what happens when the bake sale grows into a factory? If a college cafeteria's cookies became popular and the college began manufacturing them, built a massive plant and employed many people, signed a contract with a major brand to put its name on the wrappers, and incidentally performed a nominal educational function by providing confectionary classes for a few students, the bake-sale principle would vanish. If the proceeds were plowed back into the cookie business – expanding production and customer base, making better cookies, and giving a multimillion dollar salary to the boss – the college would expect to be called into question if it claimed tax-exempt status for its factory.

Somewhere between the bake-sale fundraiser and the sports extravaganzas we see on TV, a transformation occurs. As much as some people may claim that big-time college sports are still truly an amateur affair, the obvious reality is that we're watching professional teams. They bear the unmistakable features of a business. It's high time – for the college officials and the lawmakers and enforcers who have been resisting the obvious – to admit it. And embracing the truth about professionalism may make it easier to do likewise about the relative disadvantages versus advantages that big-time sports bring to the realm of higher education.

THE PICTURE WE SEE – UPSIDE AND DOWNSIDE

When the lobby for big-time sports is concerned about tax status, the discussion runs to claims about amateurism and the plea about losing money. Otherwise, the focus is on income production and entertainment value, factors associated with professionalism. The spin on finances is positive. We're told that the income

a team derives from television, ticket sales, donations from boosters, and corporate sponsorships goes not only toward defraying
the expenses that team incurs but can also be used to pay the
expenses of other teams its institution fields that are unable to
pay for themselves. At schools with successful programs, the
revenue may be enough to make the athletic department self-
sufficient and to have money left over that can be channeled into
constructing classroom buildings and laboratories, hiring professors, increasing financial aid, and other academic commitments
that critics of big-time teams would find themselves wanting to
support.

Amidst the mixed messages about losing money and making
money, where does the truth lie? Colleges with big-time teams
have done little by way of clarification. Accounting practices
vary from school to school, and it's common for many expenses,
sometimes large ones, not to be recorded against the athletics
budget but instead be charged to the physical plant, food services, tutoring, and other listings. So knowing how many teams
truly can be said to turn a profit is difficult. But fewer are likely
to than claim to, since many have avoided full disclosure of their
expenses.

The questionable accounting doesn't apply only to individual
teams, but to athletic-department budgets as well. How many of
the schools claiming their sports programs as a whole are self-suf-
ficient are to be believed? To its credit, the NCAA did a comprehensive study covering the years 2004-2009, using a standard format that included various sports-related expenses that may have
been hidden by the schools' customary accounting procedures.
Construction of facilities wasn't included, and this would have
been another major cost. But even without figuring in construction, nearly 95 percent of the 300-plus Division I athletic programs
showed a net loss, and in 2009 only 14 of the 120 playing at the
highest level in football avoided red ink. That number may vary a

bit from year to year, but it's clear that the vast majority of schools with big-time sports lose money on them.

Living on the edge of the profit margin or below it leaves athletic departments challenged to find funding. One response is to increase the amount allotted to sports from the general budget, sometimes by increasing the special fees for sports that students are required to pay   along with tuition. (A third of the schools in a 2010-2011 survey were nearing or above $500 per student per year.) Doing this provokes the ire of the many students not interested in sports and raises a question about the ethics of assessing all students to pay for the entertainment of only some. Another common response is to reduce the number of varsity athletic offerings the budget supports. Teams such as wrestling and swimming that bring in little revenue find themselves in jeopardy, and many schools have dropped them.

Schools that might be tempted to economize by moving down to small-time in sports other than the revenue-producing ones of football and basketball are prevented from doing that. NCAA regulations require an institutional minimum of six or seven men's teams and seven or eight women's teams at the Division I level in order to participate in Division I. And schools that might want to play at the top level only in lower-profile sports that are less costly to operate find they have to be there in football or basketball as well. A few exceptions are permitted, but this is the policy generally, and it's a significant cause in keeping the expense for athletics high for schools with big-time teams.

Judging by revenue intake versus expenses, big-time sports are a risky venture for higher education institutions to engage in. For return on investment, putting money into other areas of business would be more promising. Why, then, put it into sports? In some cases the answer may be that the decision makers are speculators, or that in their particular situations a team with a high profile as a winner or with boosters who can be counted on for considerable donations is a solid venture. The larger answer, though, that applies whether a big-time team turns a profit or not, is that the entertainment the team provides is valuable in other ways. It offers a series of large-scale events for students to attend that serves more of them than any other social function colleges sponsor. And it creates camaraderie among students by providing something to pull together and root for, a coherence all schools desire and that can spill over into other activities. All of this inspires a loyalty that will carry into the future when students become alumni and are asked to give back financially to their alma maters. And besides those who attend the school, the general public can join the festivities. The school provides an entertainment venue for the community at-large, and a common rallying point, while scoring a gain in town-gown relations.

Entertainment value is said to influence enrollment. High school students applying to college often put the presence of big-time sports on the list of features they look for. Schools that win major championships sometimes report surges in admissions applications for the next year. As this happens, community relations grow into public relations of a broader scope – the school's name carries through newspapers and electronic media statewide and nationally.

The factors of entertainment and public relations are not given dollar amounts and figured into budgets. They're hidden gains, it could be argued, that offset the hidden costs for sports that fail to show up in athletic-department accounting practices. And athletics budgets themselves, sports supporters assert, should be viewed in the context of the institution as a whole. The amount spent on sports teams is a small fraction compared with expenditures for teaching, research, buildings and maintenance, and so on. Unfortunately this perspective is misleading on both counts. The hidden gains may not be worth the cost, and saying that the piece of the budget that goes to sports is minimal understates the case.

To argue for the worth of by-products in any industry is chancy, particularly if their monetary value can't be established. But even if it can, creating those products may not be something an organization wants to spend its money on and would choose to put into its budget as an expenditure. When colleges benefit from the publicity sports teams bring, they're pleased, of course. Would they have spent money specifically for that publicity? Probably not.

Downplaying the significance of a particular expenditure compared with larger ones faces a similar problem – it may not be something an institution wishes to or should spend its money on at all. While it can be argued that sports are a relatively small cost in the large scheme of a college's operation, that cost may still be too much. If the school's mission is about learning – disseminating knowledge and generating knowledge – then small-time teams that follow the principles of amateurism are the only ones that fit within it. Money an institution spends beyond that mission is money that should be spent within it instead.

Still, if the portion of the budget going to sports entertainment truly is small, fighting against it on principle may not seem worth it. Just how small, then, is small? An NCAA-commissioned study shows that athletics expenses at Division I schools, on average, accounted for about 6 percent of their annual budgets in 2006. And the figure was on the rise, up from 4 percent 3 years earlier. If it stands a little higher today, and doesn't include costs such as facilities construction that colleges don't like to put into their accounting for sports, what is the figure really? Is it too much to think 10 percent or more at many schools? After all, the same NCAA data tell us that over 50 schools had already reached that mark at the time of the study, with many more close behind. With the amount of the budget spent for sports on the rise, and the likelihood that at many schools it takes up at least a tenth of the grand total, the argument for downplaying it is lost. What was meant to be an assurance for budget-watchers becomes a warning sign instead.

Beyond staking out a substantial portion of the budget, big-time sports have a negative impact on higher education in other ways. They draw in recruits who are mishandled as workers. Another NCAA study shows that Division I players in many sports, not just the money-makers, have commitments to their sports that average nearly 40 hours a week. Colleges would counsel other students working full-time jobs to take out loans and work less, or to drop to part-time status, but not so with "student-athletes." These students are paid for their labor, but their income is modest – limited to tuition and basic living expenses. As coaches' salaries and TV revenues increase in great leaps, NCAA regulations keep players' earnings from exceeding the cost of attending school. Money made by promoting their names and images – which can be substantial in some cases – goes to their schools. They receive none of it. If they quit to go to a team at another school, they're required to wait a year before being allowed to play (unless the coach they've left behind signs a waiver, which often they won't). Players who see the system as unfair have been known to take under-the-table payments and gifts from boosters, but they risk severe penalties if they get caught.

Coaches demand year-round dedication from their players. Playing seasons last for about half of the school year, sometimes with considerable time absent from campus for road trips to away games. And in the off-season players are expected to follow regular workouts. The commitment of time and energy is draining, and is a hindrance to attending class and studying. And compounding this liability for many athletes is the fact that they're a poor fit scholastically at the institutions they attend. Their academic skills are below those of the student body in general – they were admitted to their colleges because of their athletic skills and wouldn't have been admitted otherwise. Admission is often handled primarily by coaches rather than admissions or academic professionals, with the process emphasizing maximum athletic talent and minimum academic qualifications.

The NCAA requires that athletes choose a major field of study and be full-time students making steady progress toward a degree. Athletes on big-time teams often respond by enrolling in the easiest majors their schools offer. Some are attending college only because it allows them to continue with sports while gearing up for a try at the professional level, and they'll gladly leave school without a degree as soon as the pros will take them. Knowing the academic profile of their athletes and the lack of energy and enthusiasm many of them have for their coursework, colleges have instituted elaborate support systems that include "class checkers" to ensure the athletes show up for class (and sometimes walk them to class) and a cadre of professional tutors (required by the NCAA, and with their own national association) assigned only to athletes. There is a growing trend on campuses with major sports programs to devote a separate building to academic support services for athletes.

Defenders of the system say the athletes should be considered fortunate. They're compensated generously by having the opportunity to get an education for free that otherwise would cost many thousands of dollars. And in terms of sports, they're given an opportunity to play at the highest level of college competition and to prepare themselves for a try at the professional level. Critics look beyond this view to recognize that the labor of young people is being exploited for the gain of institutions and coaches. While some players may be worth only a modest salary, the more talented are underpaid, and the most talented are greatly underpaid for their performance and for the marquee power of their names. They're captive workers who are not allowed to sell their services to the highest bidder, since the colleges, in cartel fashion, have agreed to cap all players' salaries at the amount of school and basic living expenses, and to restrict the opportunity for players to change teams.

Not only does the system of big-time sports run counter to the financial best interest of many players, but so does the free education they are supposed to get. While some players progress normally toward a degree, many are overmatched in classroom settings where they struggle. They're separated from other students by their busy training schedules, and isolated by their range of majors and the academic support available only for their special-interest group. In sum, players focus too heavily on a non-academic pursuit that detracts from their being full-time, serious students, which colleges deal with by providing extreme and contorted measures of special help.

Given all of this, when they finish school by graduating or dropping out, only a few actually make it to the next level of sports as professionals. For a large number, their futures could have been better served by studying a different field or attending a different institution, perhaps a community college or trade school. The usual counter-argument here brushes off the problem by asserting that the learning gained by going to college is good for anyone, including athletes, but this misses the point that postsecondary education in general offers many sorts of learning, and individual institutions only offer some of them. And the ones they offer may not suit the needs of the athletes who are recruited to play on big-time teams. To put it another way, if high school guidance counselors were to recommend schooling for athletes based on their educational strengths and academic preparedness, we can expect that in many cases they wouldn't even consider the schools those athletes end up attending.

The repercussions athletes face are pervasive at the major college level. While football and basketball are the driving financial force and are the sports generally thought of as "big-time," other sports follow their model minus the revenue. Although they may play to small crowds, and their TV appearances will be on local channels if at all, athletes in all sports designated as Division I by the NCAA train and perform as long and hard as those in the main revenue-producing sports. They often have intentions or dreams of playing at a higher level after college – in professional leagues or in the Olympics and other national and international competitions. They have grueling travel schedules with missed classes. And they, too, are given preferential admission, and often attend schools where they find themselves mismatched in the classroom. They face difficulty in keeping up with their studies, feel pressure to choose an easy major, and have a need for special academic services. While these athletes and their sports bring in little money, their presence is considered important in enabling an institution to present an image as a leader in all it undertakes, and as addressing society's reverence for competitive athletics in a comprehensive way. That image feeds into publicity, which in turn attracts donors. It's part and parcel of the pursuit of college sports as a professional enterprise. The exploitation found in that enterprise goes beyond the confines of football and basketball. Many athletes, whose services are sponsored by their schools and are counterproductive to their being serious students, would be better off academically in a different setting.

The financial burden and exploitation of athletes that go with big-time sports make a strong case against the system. There is a third element that many critics add. They point to an anti-intellectual ethos on campus that affects the student body in general, and that ties in with a school's commitment to sports. While in broad terms this connection holds, the second part is sometimes overblown, and a fix for it is more difficult than one for finances or the treatment of athletes.

When colleges admit athletes who are bound to struggle in the classroom, and when even the ones who belong academically end up taking easy courses and majors, missing classes because they're exhausted or unprepared or on road trips, and generally putting sports before learning, the message other students take away is that the system allows for such things. Slacking on your studies is condoned, tacitly encouraged. The key to going to college is to be carried along in the classroom while focusing on life beyond. For some students that means holding a job, which is essentially what scholarship athletes do, but for others it runs to a life of leisurely diversions – watching soap operas or movies, following the rock music scene, or just hanging out. Colleges have televisions and movie showings, sponsor concerts, and provide lounges for students, but sports are the one pastime they organize for regular mass participation far beyond any other. Tens of thousands of people at big-time sports schools are packed into outdoor stadiums or indoor arenas frequently through most of the school year. And to supplement the games there are pep rallies, out-of-season practices, and awards ceremonies for smaller crowds. Attending games and rallying around the team becomes a lifestyle that competes with the proper purpose of going to college. The concern isn't simply that too much time spent being a sports fan takes time away from studying, but that the cult of being a sports fan incites a bad attitude about academics that overcomes a rightful seriousness for learning.

An extension of the critique of anti-intellectualism adds the ever-presence of alcohol to the formula. The binge drinking today's students are notorious for couples with sports in pre-game and post-game parties, and extends to any day of the week in bars as well as student housing to forge a hedonistic lifestyle that merely tolerates academics. One prominent critic has dubbed the whole affair "beer and circus," playing on the expression "bread and circuses" that famously described the stadium crowds in ancient Rome as being disconnected from serious thought. Many students take pride in having their school appear on the *Princeton Review* annual list of "Top Party Schools," established by a national poll and reported extensively by the major media. Nearly all of the names on the list are big-time sports schools. College administrators appear worried and preoccupied over excessive drinking, while tailgating parties for sports events indulge underage drinkers, and television broadcasts for their teams' games are awash in beer commercials. Sports enthusiasts may pass all of this off as healthy school spirit and youthful exuberance, but critics can't help but see inebriated fans and a degeneration of the meaning of higher learning. The advancement of knowledge loses out, replaced with other values and guided by the spectacle of big-time sports.

The presence of anti-intellectualism, spurred on by sports and drinking, is real. Simple observation of campuses around the country says so in the large number of students who embrace the pleasure principle and shun a serious work ethic. But when critics assert the moral authority to point it out, they often come off sounding haughty and narrow-minded. While the evidence is obvious, the conclusion about what's wrong can remain elusive. For one thing, relaxation and time away from studies isn't a bad thing. A certain amount of it is natural and good. And there is nothing inherently wrong with the enjoyment of spectator sports. The key for students is to know how much is enough, or too much – to recognize when healthy leisure turns into unhealthy escapism. For commentators the trick is to establish that point in a way that doesn't sound like griping by someone who has no interest in athletic performances.

The main problem, though, for the critique of sports and anti-intellectualism is that the object of concern is rooted in various sources and isn't merely sports-induced. Attitudes acquired in high school, and those promoted in the media, along with low expectations and standards in mass-production lecture courses with professors who don't engage their listeners, and the fact that today many people with marginal academic skills go to college, are only some of the other factors that feed into the unenthusiastic performance many college students give in their studies. The cult of the sports fan is a main contributor, but to a broad and complicated affair. The same qualification holds for alcohol. While partying and cheering for the team combine to bring double pleasure and double distraction from studying, partying does well on its own without sports spectacles and students who are fans. Schools with big-time sports don't have a corner on inebriation. The ones with small-time teams have party scenes that are less obvious and less publicized. They revolve around other interests and activities, and don't need the goings-on in sports venues for encouragement.

Since anti-intellectualism and drunkenness among students are much more than sports-related problems, dealing with them means looking beyond sports to get at other causes. But it doesn't mean that because the whole matter is complex, sports can't be recognized for their role and be held accountable. Sharing responsibility for a difficult predicament doesn't mean being absolved from that responsibility. What it should mean is that to whatever extent colleges can curb anti-intellectualism by curbing overindulgence in a subculture of sports, they ought to act responsibly and do that. It should happen in a way that watching sports events isn't de-legitimized as a leisure pursuit, and colleges aren't seen as imposing a fuddy-duddy regime. But a strong hand is needed to find a proper proportion for the role of sports where big-time programs have pushed it out of proportion.

A BETTER PICTURE IS POSSIBLE

The big-time approach to college sports demands an overhaul – for the good of the athletes as well as colleges' finances and the intellectual atmosphere on campus. But defenders of the system argue for the entertainment value provided to students and the school spirit and publicity that go with it, along with the chance for it to be a money maker even if it often is not. The academic and nonacademic purposes within higher education institutions bump up against one another for a result that is increasingly dysfunctional. There is, however, a way out that will give each side at least most of what it wants. One fundamental change is required, after which others fall into place. Versions of the system that results, although usually not as comprehensive as what's being proposed here, have been suggested by some of the more thoughtful critics. Teams that operate on a big-time model will be declared professional. All other teams are amateur. This two-part structure replaces the present and more complicated NCAA structure of Divisions IA, IAA, II, and III. Educational and non-educational interests are no longer tied together through nuancing – instead, they're clearly demarcated and left to follow their natural paths.

A professional team is owned by an entity outside of the school bearing its name. A coalition of alumni boosters is an obvious choice for ownership, although it might be a local business or community group. Profits go to the ownership entity, but with an arrangement for the school to get a generous share. Losses are born by the ownership entity and not by the school. Teams are free to make connections with major league professional teams for part ownership or looser sponsorship agreements. Either way, the major league teams contribute to the player development that's crucial for them and that they've long counted on colleges to bear the costs for.

Professional teams have no restrictions on how they make their money through ticket sales, TV, selling team paraphernalia, selling signage on billboards and team uniforms. And they pay income tax on their profits. They might be eligible for tax breaks if they donate to the schools they represent, since those schools are nonprofit organizations.

Ownership of athletic facilities can vary, but a stadium or arena located away from campus, or even one on campus but used mostly by a professional team, should be owned by the team or by another outside entity.

Instead of athletic scholarships, players are paid salaries negotiated according to their skill levels and to market demands. They're not required to be students at the school whose team they play for or at any other school. If they apply for admission to their team's school, no preference will be given for their status as an athlete. Players might enroll at any school that meets their educational needs, and they will probably attend classes in the off-season or on a part-time basis during the season. Teams should counsel players about what schooling is best for them and make sure scheduling of classes fits into their work schedules. Amateur players on college teams will be welcome to try out for pro teams, understanding that if they make the team, their professional commitment would require curtailing their college studies.

All teams that are not professional are designated as amateur. In accordance with true amateurism, there are no athletic scholarships or other financial compensation given for being an athlete, and playing seasons and off-season practices are carefully limited. Preference given in admission to varsity athletes, a common occurrence today even at nonscholarship schools (the NCAA's Division III), will be largely eliminated – used only in a general sense to ensure that a school's student body isn't shy on athletes and glutted with musicians, debaters, entrepreneurs, and technophiles. The point is to have students with proven skills of a certain kind who add to the extracurricular life of the campus. But athletes a college accepts for admission should fall within its academic profile of accepted students as a whole. If not, there will be an academic mismatch similar to what exists today in Division I and at some Division III schools as well. Highly selective colleges may balk at the admissions restrictions, worried they won't be able to accept enough athletes, but they'll still be able to trade on their prestige to draw academically talented ones. What they'll give up are star players who are underqualified. The admissions restriction must be written carefully into NCAA regulations, and enforced through regular reviews of colleges' admissions-office records.

Holding the line between amateur and professional is crucial. Otherwise the result will make a sham of reform by simply adding another layer of commercialism to what exists now. Teams that have tendencies beyond amateurism should join the professional ranks. Within the amateur system, schools that truly believe there is educational value in playing on a varsity team should be encouraged to field multiple teams in a given sport, according to student interest and the size of the student body.

The new system applies to all sports, not just the ones known today as revenue- producing, since all are subject to the problems of exploiting athletes and draining the budget, and in varying degrees to inspiring anti-intellectualism. Varsity athletes will use the same services as other students, with no special housing or special meals or special tutoring. Expenditures for athletics will be fully disclosed, under a uniform approach to accounting that is monitored by the NCAA.

The NCAA will abandon its commercial function. It's likely the professional teams will want to form a collectivity, and units or individuals from the present NCAA might function well there, but it needs to be entirely separate from the organization that represents amateur sports. As the NCAA's role ceases with profit-making concerns, its focus will be strictly on enforcing the rules of amateurism. There will be ample need for enforcement, as some schools and coaches accustomed to present-day practices could easily want to stretch varsity sports beyond the pattern that amateur teams are meant to follow.

The new system provides strong answers to two of the three main problems critics have rightfully decried about big-time college sports, and a partial answer to the third. Students will not be exploited by colleges for profit and publicity. Instead, professional athletes playing for school teams will be paid the large or small salaries they deserve, and they'll be free to pursue whatever schooling is best for them, while varsity athletes will be afforded the time and energy to be serious students, and will attend schools where they're a proper fit academically. Colleges will be spared the financial drain that teams built on a big-time model usually incur. While amateur teams will have to be financed, their costs are known to be much less than for the big-time teams of today. And the money spent will be for the true purpose of amateurism – providing an outlet for having fun, and promoting extracurricular learning. As for the anti-intellectual affect of big-time sports on the student body, it will continue to exist but to a lesser degree. The noxious image of the athlete as an academically unqualified slacker will be removed, and some of the impetus for a "beer and circus" lifestyle will go with it. Students will be separated from professional athletes, but the athletes will still perform to entertain them and as a potential enticement for their devotion and distraction.

On the other hand, supporters of big-time sports will also find the new system to their benefit. Professional teams will be potential moneymakers for the schools they represent, yet without the schools risking a loss of money. From an investment point of view, that arrangement is hard to resist. Students will continue to enjoy spectator sports as they do now and continue to have teams to rally around. Sports-minded alumni can still look fondly upon their pride and joy, and their school will benefit from the publicity coming from the professional teams bearing its name. Coaches for the professional teams will be free from the boondoggle of amateur rules they're now expected to follow and from the pretense that their rosters are filled with serious full-time students. Boosters will be free to give large sums of money to their professional teams without being censured for buying favor in the realm of higher education. They'll have direct control over their teams through ownership and not have to worry about conflicting with the agendas of college administrators.

Who might not welcome the new system? Some sports purists may be offended – those who maintain that an athletic team bearing a college's name should be made up only of full-time students attending that school. But is this sentiment enough to oppose direly needed reform? Faculty who have been strong opponents of big-time teams may believe too little will be done in response to sports-inspired anti-intellectualism on campus. If so, will this frustration bring about a willingness to fight for a stronger measure such as reducing big-time teams to an amateur level? How strenuously will people with this perspective want to push against a means of reform that accomplishes a fair share of what they would like to?

Another likely source of opposition are parties who are afraid they'll lose standing personally. Some present Division I coaches might fear for their jobs or a salary reduction if their teams took on new ownership. On the other hand, they'll be free to negotiate their contracts without being resented for subverting the pay scale in academia. Division II coaches will be caught between moving to amateur status and full-fledged professional status, and may fear a move downward. Division III coaches may be unhappy if they're in the habit of recruiting academically underqualified players, since the new amateur system disallows

it. The key to their success in the future is coaching the players who are a legitimate fit in the classroom rather than relying on talented athletes who are misfits there. Current non-
revenue-producing teams playing at the Division I level might
fear for financial backing in converting to professional status.
Then again, they could welcome the opportunity to go out into
the community and solicit sponsors. NCAA employees are still
another group who will be apprehensive about their future. The
organization will be reduced by losing one of its two main functions, and for the one that remains – overseeing teams that are
truly amateur – it will have to rely entirely on colleges for direct
funding instead of the present arrangement that takes a cut from
the revenue of big-time teams (primarily from the "March Madness" men's basketball tournament). NCAA employees on the
commercial side will be out of their jobs, but can hope to find
other ones in the new professional enterprise.

Major league professional teams won't like the idea that
they may be asked to pay for developing the players that colleges, until now, have developed at their own expense. But why
should higher education bear a burden that obviously belongs
elsewhere? It's quite reasonable to ask the major leagues to contribute to their own lifeblood and to welcome into the professional ranks teams that have been commercial enterprises in
every way but their tax designation. The pitch is more difficult
to nonprofit organizations, ones connected to sports like gymnastics, track and field, and swimming that don't hold the revenue potential of football and basketball. Some of these organizations are already involved with college sports – through
coaching clinics, sharing venues, for example – but they have
limited financial resources and could fear the dilemma of being
pressured to share those resources or watch the demise of teams
and decline of quality in their sports. Still, they should welcome the freedom of the newly defined professional teams to be

openly commercial, and be willing to help in locating sponsors beyond themselves.

This overview of who can be expected to favor the new structure and who can be expected to oppose it is a telling sign that adopting that structure is the right course of action. People in an enterprise that is secondary to the primary purpose of higher education, and presently an obstruction to it, will sacrifice their own personal gain, while the primary purpose is strengthened for the many it's properly meant to serve. The secondary enterprise would continue to exist in an independent form to serve its own purpose. Colleges need to be free to operate without the demands and enticements of high-functioning sports teams. The time is overdue for college officials to face up to this reality and to spin off a vastly overgrown encumbrance.

– 6 –

COLLEGE GOES TO HIGH SCHOOL

Over the last several decades American high schools have undergone an amazing transformation – they've become colleges. High school students are taught in high school classrooms by high school teachers, in courses that carry college credit. Under the banner of the AP (Advanced Placement) program, secondary schools can offer as many as they want of 37 college courses in 22 subjects. And it's common for college-bound students to enroll in them. Today, and even more so in the future, high school graduates are likely to begin higher education having already completed at least a couple of courses, with a semester's or full year's worth not unusual.

Starting college studies in high school is popular with many people. Students and parents like the advantage that a transcript bearing AP courses gives them in the college admissions process. And they especially like the idea of using AP credits to reduce the number of courses needed to graduate from college, so getting a degree becomes quicker and cheaper. Public officials concur as they look for ways to put students through college faster, thus alleviating the costs they budget for. College administrators (although they might not admit it) appreciate that AP lightens their responsibility for providing basic coursework for first- and second-year students. And college faculty (although they might not admit it) appreciate having someone else teach basic courses, so they'll be able to concentrate more on research and on teaching advanced courses in their specialties.

With this broad range of supporters seeing they can gain from AP, critics have been largely missing or ignored, although the more selective colleges have become concerned about the number of college courses their applicants claim to have completed before arriving on campus. Having watched the program's enormous growth, those schools have taken measures to restrict the AP credits they used to accept routinely. And other colleges, ones that are not as selective, are now joining them. But for the most part the practice of teaching college courses to high school students through AP rolls along as a juggernaut, adding many students as well as new high schools each year. What's happened is that a system originally designed for a small number of accomplished young people has expanded into a right of passage for secondary-level students in general, some of them not even college bound. AP now warrants careful scrutiny about its quality and its worth. Its claim to college comparability is questionable, and the practice of combining high school and college leaves the worth of the final product in doubt.

AP began a half-century ago as a cooperative effort by a group of elite colleges and high schools, including Harvard, Princeton, Swarthmore, Andover, Exeter, Lawrenceville, and others. Its purpose was to offer the brightest of high school seniors an opportunity to take a college course or two as a challenge. Soon after its inception the program came under the control of the College Board, and it built up rapidly, increasing its numbers by several fold each decade. Records of AP test-takers show there were several thousand per year in the late 1950s. The number grew to over a 100,000 by 1981. Ten years later it was 350,000, and by

2001 it had snowballed to 850,000. The million mark came in 2003, and many more students than that were actually taking AP courses. It had become common to take the courses but skip the tests, and a third of the students enrolled did that. By 2011 there were nearly 2 million test-takers, who took 3 and a half million tests.

While it would seem that the growth rate should have tailed off at some point, when fewer enclaves of the brightest remained yet to be enrolled, that didn't happen. Instead there was a change of emphasis from elitism to inclusion, and the proliferation continued. In the 1980s enrollment was opened to 11th and 10th graders, and eventually to 9th graders, and today half of all AP students are not yet high school seniors. The move toward inclusion also emphasized enrolling minority and low-income students, many of whom originally wouldn't have been considered ready for early college. The College Board's announced goal is to have AP demographics mirror those of the U.S. population. And further yet, the Board came increasingly to encourage the opening of AP to anyone wanting to participate, erasing any vestige of the notion that the program is reserved for top students. Their promotional literature has made this point clear. Many high school administrators have followed the lead, generating a competitive pressure among schools to keep up with one another in AP expansion, while they support peer pressure among students for more of them to enroll in AP courses.

The latest variation on inclusion identifies still another group of students AP is beginning to serve. Dissatisfied that standard remedial efforts haven't worked to bring up the educational level of low-performers, some schools now require all students to take at least one or two AP courses. Many will not be headed to college, but the rationale is that some may be enticed to try. Those who don't will benefit anyway from the rigors of AP – being forced to study hard, they'll gain skills and knowledge and attitudes that will help them get good jobs or get into trade schools. Using AP for remediation isn't a widespread practice, but it is growing, and the fact that it occurs at all tells us that AP is stretching toward a frontier its founders wouldn't have dreamed of.

Given all of its growth and transformation, has AP maintained the quality for which it was originally known? Or, as skeptics suspect, has it been watered down? AP supporters claim the program is successful in all of its multiple purposes, and that, in spite of constant expansion, the courses continue to be as comparable to college courses as they were in the early days of elitism and restricted enrollment. Grades on AP tests reflect this contention, having remained relatively stable over many years. Between 1991 and 2011, when the program more than quadrupled its size, and the expansion included many students who wouldn't have been considered qualified for AP in earlier times, the average test score dropped only very slightly. On a five-point scale, it went from 3.01 to 2.86. How was this steadiness accomplished? The answer enthusiasts would prefer is that the program tapped into a vast unused potential among our nation's teenagers. A strong curriculum handled by capable teachers brought out more from undistinguished students than our schools have been able to do otherwise. Nonbelievers, on the other hand, see wishful thinking, a Lake Wobegon effect where everyone is above average. They're wary that the optimistic picture is a mathematical illusion.

The College Board has always held confidently that AP's quality is college-equivalent, and over the years they have cited various research studies that acknowledge the virtues of the program. However, a circumspect look at the research reveals its limitations and challenges the claim of equivalency. Many of the studies relate participation in AP to success in college as measured by factors such as grade point average, retention, credit hours taken, and selectivity of the institutions attended. None of this tells us specifically about AP courses relative to the college courses they're supposed to substitute for. At best there is only an indirect inference. Further limitations are that some studies focus narrowly on a single institution, some haven't undergone the peer review process to ensure professional workmanship, most are based on data that today are 5 years old or more (the program has doubled in enrollment in less than 10 years), and often the self-selection effect created by variables other than taking AP isn't accounted for.

These limitations are ignored in the self-congratulatory profile AP presents to the public. Also missing is mention of evidence contrary to the good news. There are significant studies that challenge the worth of AP, including one in particular from the Harvard Science Education Department in 2007. It summarizes the weaknesses in existing research, and offers a new angle on measuring the college-equivalency of AP courses. A few of the studies favorable to AP have looked at how college students who used it to skip an introductory college course have fared in a higher level "sequential" course. The general finding has been that they fared as well as or better than students who didn't take AP and instead took the basic college course. But this apparent support is misleading. One reason is that college courses may include more and higher level material and requirements (noticeable in further testing, papers, labs, and other projects) than AP courses, where college equivalency is measured entirely through end-of-course tests. So students skipping a college course may be missing out on full treatment. Another reason is that the material taught in prerequisite courses may not relate closely to the specific higher level courses that studies have linked them with (for instance, AP English Language and Composition with an upper level literature course, AP Psychology with a psychology department course on statistics). Here is an alert that when AP students perform well in "sequent" courses they've skipped ahead to, the reason may have to do with variables other than AP.

The Harvard study avoided the problems related to sequencing. Students who were successful in AP (test score of 3, 4, or 5) but still took a basic level college course were compared with students in the same course who hadn't taken AP, with careful controls for several variables other than AP (including SAT math score and highest level high school math course taken) that can account for academic performance. The focus was on science courses only, the work was peer reviewed, and data came from 55 institutions comprising a nationally representative distribution by size, type, and level of selectivity. The upshot was that students who had scored well on AP tests did only marginally better in basic courses than students without AP. Yet the AP students had the supposed advantage of taking the college-level material twice while the non-AP students took it only once.

This finding arouses suspicion that AP has been oversold. Certainly students are learning a great deal from the courses, but is that learning really at the college level? Another key to the answer lies with the way AP test scores are validated. Before the tests are given to high school students, they're tried out on college students who have just completed a basic course. The college students' scores are used as a benchmark. At first glance this may seem like a reasonable process, but it turns out to be far from it. If the concern is to find out what group A knows relative to group B, then A should take B's test instead of B taking A's. If we want an appropriate comparison between AP students and college students, let it be done this way. Let AP students take the tests college professors give to their classes. Of course, an objection might be raised that AP students will be at a disadvantage in taking real college tests because they have studied from a different syllabus, but this same disadvantage occurs when college students take the AP tests. Professors may well suspect their students are learning more than AP students, but having them answer test questions based on a canned syllabus that's not their own will fail to show it. AP students, in contrast, have followed the AP syllabus and often have gone through extensive test prep both in class and outside, sometimes with many weeks of poring over simulated questions or real ones taken from old exams. Add to this point a concern that the college students may not be giving their best effort, since their answers aren't determining their grades, and the validation process becomes quite messy. Maybe that's why, on some of the AP tests, answering half or fewer of the questions correctly is good enough to earn college credit.

Where do we stand in rating AP as college-equivalent based on research findings? Studies its parent organization relies on are problematic for several reasons. And looking at the performance of college students on trial tests is misleading – it's based on inverted logic and stacks the deck for AP students. In spite of the raft of data the College Board can appeal to, the information that would make the case for AP's college comparability is missing. As a product assessment, the result is embarrassing. Anything like it for other industries would be considered inadequate. For all of the confidence in AP its officials display, and the statistical profile they can present to dazzle unquestioning well-wishers, skeptics' eyes see smoke and mirrors.

So much for defending AP on its merits. When that isn't working, advocates sometimes change tactics. Rather than applauding AP, they depreciate the college experience it's supposed to replace. The message is that the bar for college standards is lower than it's assumed to be, making it easier for AP to reach. The attack is on the large-lecture format colleges often employ. While a strong case can be made that students learn better in smaller groups, the argument doesn't work to turn high schools into colleges. The claims against large lectures – that they can be boring and don't provide interaction with the instructor – are true. But small classes are not immune from being boring, and while lack of interaction is a drawback, it also allows a lecturer to avoid slowing down for less prepared students, a problem AP faces because of its inclusiveness.

Whatever edge might be given to high schools over colleges because of class size is strongly overridden when two factors of greater importance are considered. The readiness of high school students to learn college material and the readiness of high school teachers to teach it tell the story. It's a huge stretch of the imagination to think that any but a tiny number of 16-, 15-, and 14-year-olds are truly ready for college study. Teenagers need time to undergo intellectual growth, just as they do physical growth. Their maturation is far greater in both ways at age eighteen or nineteen when they're in their first year of college than when they're in high school, especially before their senior year. And compounding the problem is the fact that many students now take AP courses in replacement of standard high school courses rather than taking the standard courses first. When that happens, their highest level of preparation for entering a college course is middle school. Little wonder that a third of all AP students don't take the AP tests. And what happens as a result? If they skipped a final exam in college, they would get an F for the exam and likely fail the course. Not so if they take what is supposed to be an equivalent AP course in high school.

Why does it matter if there are students enrolled in AP courses who are not ready for the intellectual rigor required to perform at the college level? What harm is done if they simply take away as much learning as they can and get high school credit but not college credit for their effort? For the students themselves, the problem is that they're not being best served through a sink-or-swim approach. Even if given extra instruction – a best case scenario that may not exist – they're being thrown into deep water prematurely, and while struggling to avoid drowning, told to do their best, and if they're lucky, thrown a life preserver. Common sense says to take them gradually through the learning process at a natural pace. This will produce better swimmers, and fewer will drown or have to rely on life preservers. Let them do college study in college – when they're ready for it.

While the struggling AP students are being ill-served, so are the ones who are truly ready. The rigor they're capable of, and that the AP label designates, is in jeopardy. The unready students will bring down the level of the class. They can't be expected to read college texts, comprehend college-level concepts, and move at a pace necessary to complete a course successfully. Teachers will feel pressured to keep them from drowning, and to do that they need to compromise college-level standards. They'll feel forced to ease up on pace and depth so the class as a whole is accommodated. The teachers will be expected to get the students through in a reasonable fashion, working with the capabilities their class rosters hold. The task teachers face will challenge even the best of them. Those who hold to standards and issue too many low and failing grades are not likely to be reappointed to AP teaching.

AP teachers themselves, a group not inclined to run down a program most of them volunteered for and consider to be a plum assignment, say they think access to their courses should be more limited than it is. In a 2008 survey by the Fordham Institute (at public schools), 70 percent of them said their AP classes are open to all comers, and two thirds said more screening is needed. Teachers are feeling the pinch of trying to teach students who aren't ready to study at the college level. But what if the students were ready? How ready are the teachers to teach at that level.? Here is another major difficulty for AP's claim of college comparability – the qualifications of the teachers. Multitudes of high school teachers are teaching courses that carry college credit. By the College Board's own estimate in 2001, there were 100,000 AP teachers, with 100,000 *new* ones needed by 2010. The Board also estimated that only one in twenty at that time held a doctoral degree, and only about half had master's degrees in the AP subjects they taught. The numbers holding advanced degrees today are unknown, but they've probably declined because expansion of the program has caused many high schools to scramble to find teachers for it. The Board's guidelines suggest a minimum of a bachelor's degree in a "content-related" field, and preference for an advanced degree.

The qualification level of AP teachers is at odds with what is expected at the college level. The vast majority of regular faculty at four-year colleges hold doctorates, while adjuncts have a minimum of a master's degree. Teaching assistants, who are employed at some schools to teach the courses AP is meant to substitute for, generally have or will soon be completing a master's degree. (Many are well beyond it.) A master's degree is the professional credential considered to be the minimum for community college teachers. If we consider the AP program to be a large lower-division college, which is precisely how it functions, what would we expect an accrediting agency to say about the acceptability of its faculty's credentials? Shaky, at best, for a community college. For a four-year institution how could the answer be anything but "unacceptable?" And what about the colleges themselves? What can their take be on the people who teach the lower division courses they routinely give credit for through AP? They would refuse to hire many of the same people to teach on their campuses.

The claim that AP is comparable to college study is seriously in doubt. But beyond that problem lies another one of a different sort. Not only is the level of instruction in question, but also the effect the program has on the amount of learning students get by the time they finish college. Is the process of acceleration AP represents – condensing high school and college by skipping over certain courses – pedagogically sound?

Even if AP were living up to its billing, and our high schools truly were capable of functioning as higher education institutions, the model of early college it puts into play leaves college graduates with a less complete education than they would have otherwise. When AP credits are used to fulfill college degree requirements, those credits are doing double duty, since they've already been used to earn a high school diploma. Colleges often have restrictive policies that prevent courses from fulfilling the requirements for more than one degree. The same course could not apply toward a bachelor's degree and then toward a master's degree, for instance. The reasoning is that neither degree should be shortchanged in the amount of learning it represents. A consistent application of this policy would mean denying credit for AP courses unless they were taken over and above the requirements for high school graduation. With students today routinely taking AP in replacement for standard high school courses rather than in addition to them, many AP credits would be denied at the college level.

College officials seem to forget their own policies, or to look the other way, as they allow AP to do double duty. As a result, when students use AP credit to reduce the number of courses they take in college, they're losing out on the accumulated learning they would have gained otherwise. When several AP courses are involved, the missed opportunity for learning is substantial. Consider two students. One takes AP English Literature, and because it transfers for college credit, decides not to take another course in literature while in college. The other student takes honors English in high school, which is only a bit less rigorous than AP, and then takes a literature course in college to fulfill a basic requirement. The second student will have read about twice as much literature as the first and have spent twice as much time analyzing it. The second student will have a more extensive education when all is said and done.

Add to the first student's high school transcript an AP U.S. history course as a junior and AP economics as a senior, which are used to fulfill the social science distribution requirement in college and get on quickly to specialized courses in a major. The second student takes honors high school courses in the same subjects and then takes two social science courses in college, perhaps in history and economics, or political science or sociology. The second student is building a deeper and more well rounded education than the first, who is rejecting that in a push to accelerate. While the first student can be said to have reached as high vertically in certain areas as the second – completing the level of a basic college literature course and two basic social science courses – the second student has reached much further laterally. It should go without saying that a sound education pushes in both directions. This point can be extended from the humanities and social sciences to the natural sciences as well, although in foreign languages and to some degree in mathematics, an argument could be made that the subject matter is more vertical and less lateral than in other disciplines. But clearly, when colleges allow students to use AP credit to accelerate, their graduates who do so emerge with a less complete package of secondary and higher education than students who don't use AP credits in this way.

Awarding college credit for AP is based on a simple vertical model of learning. It's this model that allows students to condense what would otherwise be two courses in the same subject – one in high school and one in college – into one course and to accelerate progress toward a degree. It can be argued that this process is economical and avoids needless repetition, and that it shows respect for students who work had to move forward. A student who takes AP American History in high school, for example, if denied college credit for it, might then take a survey course in the same subject as a college freshman. In fact, the survey might be a prerequisite for any higher courses in that field. Why require the repetition?

The question is often asked in a rhetorical way, with the assumption that repetition is an unnecessary burden that should be avoided. In fact, repetition is a key element in learning, a method that can be planned and worked into the curriculum. It reinforces essential knowledge, fixes it into place. When students see material they're familiar with, they won't need as much time with it as they did on their first encounter. A college course can move more quickly over the basics that high school courses need greater time to dwell on – in American history, for example, the details of wars, the platforms of political parties and labor movements and civil rights groups, the tenets of the U.S. Constitution, and so on. Then it goes to a deeper level, a more sophisticated understanding of the subject. That depth may involve greater discussion of the causes for wars, the philosophical principles underlying various parties and movements, and challenges to the U.S. Constitution, and it may involve as well a significant amount of reading from primary documents. Just as high school study is positioned to do more than the middle school study that precedes it in the same subjects (middle school does teach some of the basics of American history), college is positioned to do more than high school. A properly conceived vertical model includes repetition as a positive factor rather than a wasteful one, and also includes the key principle of depth built upon the repetition.

AP advocates seem to pay little heed to the liability of acceleration, just as they seem unaware that the data-laden picture the program's handlers present is overly rosy. But in recent years cracks of another sort have arisen in the facade that demand attention – high schools have devised advanced courses that deviate from AP. In 2007 the College Board conducted a nationwide audit of all courses bearing the AP label. There were many reports of schools using it to enhance their reputations by attaching it to courses that didn't live up to expected AP content. When the syllabi were reviewed, a third of them were found lacking. The rejected ones were either revised or no longer called AP. AP's growth invited a major abuse of the program – interlopers that don't belong. To their credit, AP's overseers rectified the situation. Unfortunately, course content is only one of the three main components in learning, the others being students and teachers. Unless those two components are controlled for as well, ensuring there is a solid syllabus won't create a college-level enterprise.

Difficulties over course content also have come from another direction. While the College Board has dropped courses at status-seeking schools for improperly borrowing the AP label, a growing number of highly respected schools have dropped AP. Some others like them never had the program, or haven't for a long time. At least several dozen respected schools are involved, mostly private but some public. Instead of AP, they offer advanced courses designed by their own faculty and not aimed at passing AP tests. These schools routinely send many of their graduates to top colleges, and they say acceptances haven't suffered without AP. Admissions offices seem satisfied that they have sufficient information from other sources. The effect the withdrawal of these schools has on overall AP enrollment is small, but the example it sets of rebellion and a "we can do better" attitude is something to be watched. An especially important factor to be recognized is the willingness the non-AP schools have for their students not to amass college credits before enrolling in college. The students can take the AP tests if they like, but they have to prepare for them on their own. Their advanced high school courses are meant to get them ready for the higher level they'll find in college, rather than substitute for it.

Where to Go From Here

Given that many of the high school students enrolled in AP today have questionable capability to do college-level work, and that the credentials of the AP teaching corps overall are well below college standards, and that the statistical data offered to support the claim that AP is college-comparable are unconvincing, what can be done to ensure that AP courses operate at the level claimed for them as worthy of college credit? A major first step is for high schools offering AP to undergo accreditation according to the standards applied to colleges. Colleges commonly stipulate that any transfer credit they award must come from institutions accredited by one of the six regional accrediting agencies authorized by the federal government – Middle States, Southern, and so on. If high schools are functioning as colleges, in order to have their courses recognized for college credit, they should meet the same stipulation. To be consistent with their longstanding practices, colleges should require that they do. Logistically there is already a connection, since the agencies that accredit colleges are the same ones that accredit high schools to operate at the secondary level. As an additional step in the process, the high schools wanting to function as colleges could ask for review by college standards.

As a part of accreditation, high schools would have to be more selective about who takes AP courses. The practice that was followed when the program was in its early years and earned a favorable reputation provides a precedent. Students should have taken the next lower course in a subject before taking AP, such as honors or regular chemistry before AP chemistry, honors or regular world history before taking AP world history. This means most AP students would be seniors by the time they're ready for AP. If not, it could be required that they be seniors. And it should be required that they be top students. Otherwise colleges are being asked to believe and certify that many of the same students they teach as freshmen, had they been on their campuses when they were fifteen or sixteen years old, would have been ready to perform then as well as they do at college age.

High schools should also be more selective about the teachers entrusted to teach AP. It's reasonable to expect them to meet the same standards they would meet if being hired at a college. A master's degree in the subject being taught should be required, or, in a rare exception, substantial and documented equivalent content knowledge. Having extensive teaching experience in high school is not a reason to make an exception, since it doesn't speak to having appropriate content knowledge. Being experienced in the classroom can't make up for lacking a background in subject matter that colleges deem minimal for their faculty. If high schools don't have qualified teachers among their full-time employees, they should hire part-timers who are qualified. Otherwise they should do what colleges do when they're unable to find a qualified instructor for a course – not offer it.

A further measure to improve AP is for new comparability studies to be conducted. Their sponsorship should be independent of the College Board, but with cooperation from the Board. In order to satisfy critics of AP, critics should be among those involved in planning the methodology of the studies and interpreting the results. When it comes to administering AP tests to college students and measuring AP students against the results, the practice should be changed. It should be balanced or replaced by having the AP students take actual college final exams that would be graded by college professors. This is the only way to remove the advantage AP students now have of extensive test prep for their own test.

If these proposals are carried out, AP will be reduced to a fraction of its present size. But the college-equivalency it claims, and that for so many reasons is seriously suspect, will be ensured. Colleges should demand it and should revise their policies to say that AP credit will be awarded only for those courses where all of the necessary conditions have been met. An easier alternative, especially if it's difficult to ensure the strict conditions for accreditation and research are accounted for, is to refuse AP credit altogether. If colleges do this en mass, the program will be left to survive on its merits as a rigorous high school curriculum. High schools can still use AP guidelines in designing their advanced courses if they choose to. College admissions officers will still be impressed when they see AP on applicants' transcripts. And in a major gain for the quality of schooling, the problem of compressing high school and college by having courses count toward both will be gone. But if students still want a leg up as they enter college, through credit for prior learning or simply for placement without credit in courses beyond the introductory level, and colleges want to give it to them, they can be tested when they arrive on campus for freshman orientation. Many colleges already do this in math and foreign languages. Other subjects can be added to allow students to take final exams from the courses they want to pass out of, with the grading done by the school's own faculty. This will mean more work for the faculty, but it's a reasonable price to pay as part of an overall effort to ensure that the credits students are awarded are truly for college-level learning.

QUADRUPLE WHAMMY ON THE CURRICULUM

Basic study of the liberal arts today is like eating at a smorgas-bord. So we're told by a commonly heard expression for describing the general education program all students take as the foundation for a college degree. Several categories of knowledge are identified that are essential to intellectual nourishment, and to go with them students are offered long lists of courses full of eye-catching titles. They're trusted to let their taste guide them in selecting a course or two from each category. One person's choices may be far differ-ent from another's, but the idea is that it's best for them to sample things as they like, and as long as they sample from each category, their acquisition of basic knowledge is taken care of. The smorgas-bord, officially called the "distribution" approach, is often dressed up by adding a required course in writing and one in math, and other features like first-year seminars, service learning, and cap-stone learning. But none of that changes its essential makeup as a spacious offering of variety and choice.

The vast majority of colleges follow this model – 80 per-cent according to a recent survey. Unfortunately it's as flawed as it is popular, leaving many students with a plateful of chef's specialty courses on narrow or unconventional subjects. It stands in opposition to a curriculum designed to cover a broad and significant range of content through a specified set of courses, such as surveys of the history of the U.S. and Western civilization, basic economics and psychology, American government, great literature, biology, and physics. These offerings are usually on the schedule, but they compete with a wide assortment of alternatives that can be chosen instead. At many schools, particularly the larger ones that educate a majority share of our nation's college clientele, students end up studying pre-Columbian cultures, non-Western cultures, criminology, advertising, foundations of education, sexuality, racism, aging, Gothic novels, children's literature, food science, the insect world, exercise science, jazz, cinema, photography, and a range of other possibilities, as the foundation for their college degrees. As a result, graduates emerge with hodgepodge transcripts that hold the evidence as to why they're embarrassingly undereducated.

Why does the system work this way? Doesn't common sense say to teach the foundation first and leave the rest for later? And to not try to substitute a patchwork made from the rest for the foundation itself? Unfortunately, common sense doesn't prevail in general education. The reason for this has a simple answer and a complicated one. The simple one is that the freedom offered by the smorgasbord is enticing. Students like courses that sound like they're fun or trendy or easy, and tend to pass up ones that are more onerous but make for a better education. Faculty like to teach their specializations rather than the basics. And administrators like to keep students and faculty happy. When reformers suggest shrinking the course lists back toward a core of essential learning, they face a stout wall of resistance. The smorgasbord is like a government entitlement program that's hard to get rid of no matter how badly it's working.

The overseers of the system, of course, don't like to admit it's working badly. They say students learn the basics in high school, and college is for advancing beyond that point. Besides, the ones who want more of the same can have it – the smorgasbord includes traditional survey courses along with the other offerings. But the troubling truth is that college students have a poor grasp of the material the survey courses teach. What they learned in high school wasn't enough, or it didn't stick. We know this from national surveys done every few years as they're finishing their bachelor's degrees. The majority of them are lost when they encounter the staples of cultural literacy – identifying the Magna Carta, Roe v. Wade, inflation, major religions, countries by continent, how many U.S. Senators there are, as only a few examples. And they're just as weak on the skills of reading, writing, critical thinking, and quantitative thinking. By one assessment fewer than half can follow the reasoning in newspaper editorials, interpret documents with tables and charts, and use simple computations to compare loan offers and food prices. Another assessment adds writing to the mix, finding that nearly half of students at four-year colleges show no improvement on basic skills after two years, a third show none at graduation, and for the ones with improvement it's minimal. These are not isolated examples of anecdotal evidence. They represent the population of new college graduates throughout the country. Much of the fundamental learning they should have gotten somewhere along the way – in high school or in college – is missing.

As for the claim that students can take courses in the basics if they want to, it overstates the case. Those courses may easily be filled up by people wanting them for their intended majors, or they may be available only in a single section at a time that creates scheduling conflicts. So while foundational learning does get space in the curriculum, the way it's done leaves its perceived worth in doubt. Simply by setting out a smorgasbord full of specialty items, colleges are telling students that many courses have equivalent worth to the well-known basics. If the people in charge don't believe in the equivalence, they go along with it anyway. They're drawn by another enticement for accepting the distribution approach to general education – it allows schools to justify staffing academic departments in fields that have few students majoring in them. Research-oriented institutions like this because they can diversify their research power and gain more prestige for comprehensiveness. Smaller schools like having departments and majors and course offerings they would forgo without the enrollment that comes from being part of the smorgasbord. Diversifying what counts as the "general" portion of undergraduate studies serves the interest of the larger academic whole.

The simple explanation, in sum, for the dominance of the smorgasbord curriculum is that it supports an administrative agenda. It's a convenient way to please students and faculty as well as to enlarge the academic landscape. But there is much more to favor it that comes from a different direction. It's not merely an opportunistic device, but it finds backing on intellectual grounds. The complicated explanation is that when the keepers of the curriculum debate its merits and justify its structure, they draw upon popular trends in the theory of knowledge. Knowledge is what students are in college to obtain, and understanding its nature is crucial for determining how to arrange it and put it at their disposal. Four key ideas hold sway in an epistemological perspective that favors the looseness and freedom of the distribution structure – that knowledge is relative and there is no one basic knowledge everyone should possess, that knowledge is imbued with politics and the curriculum should be too, that learning *how* to think is more important than learning *what* to think, and that the explosion of new knowledge in recent times makes trying to teach a broad-ranging curriculum futile. These ideas are interrelated, yet they also stand on their own. They're not new, and while some have more history than others, they're all in vogue today. They have an initial attractiveness about them, an aura of sensibility, but they've been overplayed and misapplied. Taken collectively, their strength has thrown a powerful whammy on common-sense thinking about general education.

Relativism

For many intellectuals today, thinking in relativist terms is a staple feature. It's common especially on college campuses. Relativism denies that knowledge can be certain or universal. True and false, right and wrong, objectivity, and rationality are myths, at least in an unequivocal sense. Knowledge is said to be conditional – it varies according to the conditions of the knower. To put it in slightly different terms, knowledge is contextual rather than absolute, meaning it will be different when approached from one perspective than when approached from another. To make a claim about truth or right is no more than to say that it's based on the point of view or context the knower starts with. And when knowers influenced by different conditions disagree, there is no essence above them or foundation below them to appeal to for guidance.

This idea has a long history tracing to the ancient world, with various forerunners of the contemporary version appearing over the centuries, although its proponents were a small minority who were likely to be considered eccentrics or heretics. During the 20th century it gained ground, and during the last few decades it has been not only acceptable but fashionable to embrace the idea that knowledge is relative. It can be found as a major player in philosophy as well as in the social sciences, the arts, literature, linguistics, and even natural science. Acceptance of relativism was fueled by intellectual movements such as Freudianism, Marxism, and structuralism, which push home the point that the contents of the mind are conditioned by internal or external forces, and by pragmatism and historicism, which support the open-ended or uncertain nature of knowledge. More recently the rage has been in "critical theory" and, especially, "postmodernism." Leading names identified with postmodernism carry marquee power in academia (Jacques Derrida, Michel Foucault, Richard Rorty, Stanley Fish, and others), although they're mostly unknown in the world outside, and some of them have had reservations about attempts by admirers to popularize and apply their ideas. The ultimate factor drawing them under the same umbrella underscores that we're all captives within our contexts, and that there are no universal standards that reside outside of contexts to act as arbiters when contexts collide with one another.

Relativism, as a principle, isn't built directly into the structure of the college curriculum. There is no general education category for it, and curriculum designers typically don't cite it as one of the conceptual tools they use. But it's there more loosely, in the background, exerting its influence indirectly. It operates against the idea of teaching a basic, uniform sort of knowledge.

If knowledge is relative, then so are determinations about what there is that's so fundamental as to mean all students should learn it. When faculty members disagree about what the basic content of liberal arts learning should be, there is no intellectual seat of higher authority to appeal to. Here is an invitation for the overseers of the curriculum to sanction the existence of a wide range of subject matter. If they have respect for the relativism of knowledge, they'll ensure that faculty voices of differing sorts are represented. Each gets its own course or courses. And since students can't possibly take all of the courses that are created, they have to choose among them. The principle of relativism supports the smorgasbord approach to general education. It's consistent with the practice of piling course after course onto the lists students select from to learn the "basics." It offers no means or reason for limiting the list. Instead, it seems to justify that the proliferation should continue as long as professors come up with new claims about what they happen to think is important. And in broader terms, relativism encourages the spawning of new contexts that emphasize still more and different ways of seeing the world – there is no means of quality control, no basis for determining what's more worthy and what's less worthy.

The problem with relativism philosophically is that it's inherently inconsistent. It becomes self-refuting. The claim that knowledge is relative is itself a knowledge claim, so by its own logic, it, too, is relative. It can't be asserted as a truth, only as a point of view or an opinion. Relativists have looked for a way to wiggle out of this predicament by saying the contextual nature of their own views is evidence of the contextual nature of all knowledge, and once this is admitted, the important thing is to try to develop convincing reasons for what to believe in without relying on the notion of universalism in the background. But this maneuver still leaves relativism stuck with the status of being a mere theory and not a truth. It does suggest that relativists realize they have to live in the real world outside of armchair theorizing, and that when they do, they have to make choices based on one belief over another. But, to be consistent with their own thinking, they're disallowed from having an ultimate basis to rely on in doing that.

Relativism can act as a positive force by opposing intolerance and by recognizing and respecting contrary points of view. It promotes a spirit of openness, widens outlooks to include new ideas and new people. So far, so good. But when closure is needed, when it's time to step back from openness and make choices, relativism not only offers no help, but it stands as a force of resistance. This difficulty shows up glaringly in moral affairs when committed relativists find themselves opposed absolutely to certain kinds of human behavior – human sacrifice, slavery, infanticide, pedophilia, to name only some, and adamantly against any justification for them. But the inconsistency of believing in relativism except when it's inconvenient seems to get lost in other situations, and the theory still holds its force. It hovers in the background in much of academic thinking, supporting an intellectual version of "live and let live." It does that in a way that goes beyond mere collegiality. It functions as a high-minded ideal, a deep mentality that justifies new ways of seeing things but refuses to judge them. When relativism is applied to the curriculum, it leads away from making hard choices about what knowledge is most important for students to have, and leaves it up to the students' own meager understanding to figure things out for themselves.

POLITICS

Politics looms large in higher education today. The great concern is for what supporters call "multiculturalism" or "diversity," and critics often denounce as identity politics or political correctness. The new politics came with the civil rights movement of the latter 20th century, and grew to the point where today it influences admissions policies and the hiring and promotion of faculty, speech codes and sexual harassment policies, and the kinds of extracurricular programming students are exposed to. The formal curriculum has been affected too. Many new courses as well as new distribution categories have been designed to align with the new politics, and their force has grown to be considerable.

Just what the new approach means can be confusing, since it comes with varying degrees of intensity, but it could be summed up as the politics of difference. Simply put, it challenges traditional ways of thinking in our society about our own culture vis-à-vis other cultures, and about the treatment of race, class, gender, and sexual orientation within our own. The idea is that culture is "multi" or plural, while traditional thinking, on the other hand, tends to privilege one culture (Western) and one element within it (white, upper-class, male, heterosexual). In its softer form the challenge says we should give greater recognition and respect to non-Western cultures and to minorities, women, gays, and the economically disadvantaged. In its stronger form it moves to the radical side of left-wing politics, and becomes a bitter indictment of Western and especially American culture as racist, sexist, homophobic, and corruptly capitalist and colonialist. It can be anything from an aware social conscience to a driven "us-against-them" resistance movement.

The politicization of the curriculum toward diversity gets a boost from relativism in claiming academic legitimacy. New ways of thinking are provided with status and given space in the curriculum. Traditional thinking comes to be regarded as less than universal, less than the final word, as being required to share the intellectual spotlight with other points of view. Another connection between diversity and relativism is the notion that knowledge is fundamentally contextual. Diversity (in its stronger form) adds that context is strongly political, meaning that politics are at the very heart of how we think about things – knowledge is colored by or controlled by background political concerns. If knowledge is suffused with politics, then the curriculum should be too. The purpose or emphasis of education moves away from teaching the basics of the various disciplines where learners acquire traditional knowledge so they can function successfully in our society as it stands now. The revised emphasis is on teaching difference, which will change society by accepting non-Western ways within our cultural practices and by combating racism, sexism, homophobia and class prejudice.

Diversity plugs into the curriculum in several ways. Many colleges have established departments or programs of ethnic studies (African-American, Hispanic-American, Asian-American), women's studies, and gender and sexuality studies (lesbian, gay, bisexual, and transgender) that offer majors and minors, and courses for the student body at-large. This means diversity has risen to have a similar status to traditional knowledge – it now holds disciplinary or quasi-disciplinary standing. Along with mathematics, English, and psychology, we find gender, ethnicity, and sexuality being treated as if they are among the basic building blocks of learning. And that status brings with it a call for inclusion in general education. It's now common for colleges to have categories or requirements within their smorgasbord structures that are dedicated to the politics of difference, with headings such as "Pluralism," "Global Knowledge," "Social and Cultural Diversity," or simply "Diversity." Some schools have two categories, one for other cultures and one for U.S. diversity, while other schools combine them into one. Just as with the rest of the categories, students take a course or two from lists of various possibilities. Some of the courses would be considered mainstream, like "Cultural Anthropology" or "Eastern Philosophy," but many are blatant challenges to tradition with titles like "Politics of Identity," "Lesbian Sex and Politics in the U.S.," "Queer Mobilities," and "Race, Gender, and Media."

Not only are these courses promoted through the creation of diversity categories, but they've had an even greater effect on general education by showing up at many colleges on the lists of courses for other categories. Courses about other cultures, women's studies, and ethnic studies often can be taken instead of traditional ones in political science, psychology, literature, history, music, and the rest of the social sciences, humanities, and arts. Even if students prefer to take traditional course work, they may find diversity offerings occupying a large share of what's available at registration and that the basic liberal learning they want is hard to get.

Further still, diversity has been incorporated into courses with traditional titles. A course on great political theorists might now include feminist writings by Mary Wollstonecraft and Simone de Beauvoir. At a greater remove from tradition, a course on Shakespeare might be taught from a feminist perspective that emphasizes the role of women in his plays and his attitude about gender and sexuality. A basic course on the history of western civilization may enlarge its lens on the connections between the West and other cultures, and again at a further remove, it might be taught as an expose of European and American imperialism and racism. Revision of this sort has occurred at colleges throughout the country. At many of them the administration has encouraged it as being in step with the times, and major grant-making organizations have provided financial support for curriculum-revision projects. The politics of diversity has become mainstream enough that it appears in many courses where its presence is unsuspected without seeing the syllabus or visiting the classroom.

The inclusion of diversity in the curriculum, in its softer form, is beneficial. With our lives today being influenced by people and places throughout the world, it's good for students to learn about non-Western cultures. And it's good for them to learn about the politics of race, class, gender, and sexuality. This learning belongs as an element of their general education programs. But how much of it? For all that exposure to difference – as found outside the Western-American tradition and within it – is good, there is proper cause for limiting it. To start with, there are reasons for giving preference to our own culture. One is simply that it's ours. It's the culture the vast majority of American college students will live in after college. They should be conversant with their surroundings, and general education should recognize this and prepare them for it. Another reason is that our culture has a high degree of accomplishment. Without being arrogant, and without denying that we have weaknesses, we should recognize that Western culture, and often the American version of it, is sought after by the people of other cultures. They desire to have our ways and achievements, even if they show hostility to some of them. Diversity advocates sometimes think in terms of leveling the field, for instance, teaching history from a global perspective and giving each of the major world cultures roughly equal time. This approach fails to value the excellence of our own culture as well as the practical importance of being familiar with it.

It's precisely the notion of our culture's excellence, though, that the domestic side of diversity means to challenge. Its purpose is to point out the existence of several forms of social inequality in our lives, and to move toward correcting them. People who believe that knowledge is inextricably political, and that race, class, gender, and sexuality are the most important matters in politics, will look for ways to put a considerable amount of diversity into the curriculum. People who believe otherwise – that only some knowledge is political, that social inequality is only part of the political, that recognizing difference is important but recognizing unity is more so – will limit the presence of the new politics. The "human studies" area of the curriculum – the social sciences, humanities, and arts, where the new politics fits – covers a vast expanse of knowledge. Human beings are much more than their race, gender, sexuality, and economic standing. We're creatures of sensation, emotion, desire, will, of expression through physical movement, and through presentations of shapes and colors and sounds of harmony and discord. Our interpersonal and ethical being involves

such things as love, friendship, duty, courage, honor, on the virtu-
ous side, and our vices aren't limited to social injustice but also run
to overindulgence, hubris, violence, bureaucratic corruption, and
beyond. Within the study of our basic beliefs – our philosophical
and religious thinking – there are more perspectives than simply
the social justice of the new politics. With all of this complexity in
the grand scheme of things, the importance of social inequality
shouldn't be overestimated. College should be a place where the
major social problems of our time are discussed, and there should
be room in the general education curriculum for that. But there
is much more to what makes people tick, and how we behave and
express ourselves, and it should carry much more weight.

In a typical general education program, perhaps six to eight
courses are slated for areas where diversity has an influence –
social sciences, humanities, the arts, writing (writing instructors
sometimes emphasize diversity themes). If there is a required
diversity course, and diversity occasionally comes into the content
of some of the other courses, then the mix with traditional learning is reasonable. When the mix goes beyond that, an undesirable
imbalance is in the making. Attention is diverted from the broad
expanse of basic knowledge and becomes overly-concentrated on
just one element of it. When the diversity requirement goes to
two courses, when diversity courses substitute for traditional ones
and swell the lists in the traditional categories, and when diversity
courses masquerade under traditional titles, the result can easily
mean that half or more of a student's basic liberal arts learning in
the human studies is spent on non-Western and race, class, gender, and sexuality concerns. The imbalance doesn't characterize all
schools. At some, diversity isn't included in general education, but
most require at least one course, and two seems to be a growing
trend. And at many the greatest influence of diversity in the curriculum is through the volume of courses it holds in the standard
categories of learning – courses that students choose instead of

American history, basic psychology, basic economics, and other fundamentals of general knowledge.

So diversity presents a danger for general education by annexing curriculum space beyond what it warrants. But there's more – the danger continues in a potentially greater way that isn't as visible. The stronger version of diversity creates hostility toward traditional knowledge. It can sour students' attitudes about the worth of the great intellectual and cultural legacy that centuries have built up and endowed us with. It teaches our next generation to see life mainly in narrowly defined political terms. If through their basic studies, they learn to conceive our tradition mainly as a chronicle of corruption (American and Western culture as the evil overlord), they'll be encouraged to look down on the knowledge that defines it. They'll think of it as regressive. This mindset, if it's carried through as a factor determining what other courses they take in college, and beyond college as a lingering taint in lifelong learning, will have an unfortunate effect on the way people pattern their lives. They won't only miss out on the content of traditional learning, but they'll do it by choice, having absorbed a narrow prejudice about it that prevents them from recognizing the importance of what they're missing, and because of this keeps them from seeking it out. General education is the foundation for shaping students' overall knowledge. When overemphasis on negative thinking about our own culture becomes the mainstay of what is "general," the result is not only narrow but grossly distorted learning.

THE PROCESS/CONTENT DISTINCTION

Educational theorists make a distinction between teaching content and teaching process. This idea has been identified with the progressive education movement for over a hundred years. It found intellectual support from educational psychologists in the 1960s, and continued into the 21st century Harvard college catalog. Content refers to the "what" of things – facts, places, terminology, events, and theories, such as 1939-1945, turbine, FDIC, Ramadan, quixotic, the Reformation, arachnid, Betty Friedan, adagio, golden mean, Santo Domingo, Monet, Keynesian, Monroe Doctrine, doublethink, rococo, cloture, isotope, Woodstock, postmodernism, Kurdistan, begging the question, Charlemagne, free will, Manhattan Project, W.E.B. Du Bois, existentialism, *Bhagavad Gita*, Ethiopia, behaviorism, Genghis Khan, St. Lawrence River, semiconductor, *A Midsummer Night's Dream*, J. Edgar Hoover, Socratic method, Reconstruction, 1st Amendment, 5th Amendment, 14th Amendment, isobar, metronome, Marxism, laissez-faire, Helen of Troy, Hermitage museum. This is a tiny sampling of content knowledge a student might learn about in the general education portion of a college degree. The list could go on and on.

Process, on the other hand, refers to knowledge of a "how to" sort – the skills of writing and computation, and the mentality that is sometimes described generically as "critical thinking." It's recognized that there are different ways to approach critical thinking and that each of the main divisions of knowledge has its own way – its own pattern of ideas and a certain methodology or set of exercises it employs. So students need to learn how historians operate, how to read a novel to get the most out of the experience, how artists deal with the human condition, how scientists arrive at the claims they make. Learning about process and about content go hand-in-hand, but learning about a given process can be accomplished without a commitment to a specific content. Students can learn effective writing or mathematical problem solving through practicing those skills in connection with any of a variety of subjects. And with the processes that are bound to certain disciplines, wide latitude still exists within a discipline. Learning about the mindset and methods of historians can be done by taking a course on Chinese history or one on the history of the Caribbean or the history of American cinema as easily as by taking a basic survey of U.S. history. Similarly, the ways of science can be learned by taking general biology or marine biology, or general physics or a specialized course on the solar system.

Curriculum designers have applied the process/content distinction to the general education curriculum in a way that supports the smorgasbord structure. Since the skills of writing and math are separable from any particular content, teaching them can be concentrated in specific courses designated for that purpose. When the subject matter involved is discipline-specific, emphasis moves away from covering a lot of territory, such as the expanse of U.S. history, a survey of great literature, or the most important laws and principles associated with the biological sciences and physical sciences. Professors can concentrate and condense by keying on any particular time and place, or writer, or any particular science or area within it, and still have students learn what they need to know about ways of thinking. Colleges can say they provide excellence in general education, but without putting students through the long, arduous experience involved in practicing basic skills in course after course, or trying to cover the basics of content knowledge in the various disciplines. As long as students take their prescribed skills courses and a course or two in each discipline (whatever those courses are), they'll have acquired the general education they need.

One problem resulting from the process/content distinction is that professors often fail to live up to the claim that they're teaching process. The writing process, in particular, gets short shrift. Many professors simply avoid it. They treat it like any of the other processes that general education is supposed to develop through a limited encounter. There's a required course for all students in

English composition, and many schools also require a couple of more courses that are specifically designated as "writing intensive." These followup courses might be in any subject, and they carry the instructor's guarantee to assign a substantial amount of writing and to grade it for mechanics and style as well as for content. Many students get little or no true writing instruction beyond this in four years of college. What about all of the rest of the courses? In some of them no writing is assigned, and grading is based on short answer tests. In many courses writing is assigned, but without the professors grading it in a way that will help students improve their writing skills. They grade for content but not process. They may circle a misspelled word here and there, or insert a comma, and they may write a general comment at the end of the paper to the effect that the writing needs work. Otherwise, they don't put in the time or effort to do what needs to be done to improve student writing – find the stylistic and technical faults and mark them, suggest moving content around and changing points of emphasis, give low grades for poor writing, and offer individual office time to students to go over problem spots, followed by a suggestion to rewrite the assignment. That's the only way students can develop the skill of writing to any appreciable degree. They need continued practice that is carefully critiqued. Some need it throughout four years of college, while others will master the technique sooner. This is an aspect of general education that should be carried on even in courses otherwise dedicated to teaching the specialized content of a major. Unfortunately students get little of it in their general education courses, no less in other courses.

Two qualifying points are needed here. One is that professors shouldn't be expected to give remedial help to students who aren't writing at the college level. Remediation belongs elsewhere. But there are many students whose work is passable but weak, and who need considerable practice to improve. The other point is that some professors, in fact, do give that practice by assigning papers and grading them diligently. The indictment doesn't belong to all faculty but to many.

Colleges are well aware that their students need more work on writing skills, and they've mounted a double-pronged effort for improvement. Writing centers staffed with specialists can be found at nearly every school to provide help at the remedial level, and occasionally other levels as well. But their size and reach is limited. To expand the centers would be expensive, and it would reinforce the notion that the proper role for professors is to teach their own disciplines while they leave the teaching of writing to a cadre of skilled technicians. And relying on technicians would isolate the mechanics of writing from the faculty's expertise with content and specific ways of presenting it such as scientific reports, poetry, business reports, argumentative essays, and journalistic pieces.

In an effort to get more professors involved, many schools have implemented "writing across the curriculum." This means recognizing that since the process of writing isn't discipline-specific, but instead spans the various disciplines, those disciplines share responsibility in teaching it. Typically a committee is set up with representatives from several fields as well as sponsorship or consultation from the English department. The committee offers suggestions and makes overtures to the various departments to assign and grade more writing. However, participation is largely voluntary, and departments might respond simply by adding another "writing intensive" course to their long lists of courses that are not of that type. Although colleges may speak proudly about having writing-across-the-curriculum programs, the net effect of those programs is questionable. They're a step in the right direction. But they face strong resistance from faculty who, even if they agree that departments besides English are responsible for teaching writing, won't take on the job personally. Many other faculty believe, and if pressed they'll argue, that it's not their job to

QUADRUPLE WHAMMY ON THE CURRICULUM

teach writing. They forget that writing is an integral part of what they themselves do in performing within their disciplines, and therefore something students in their disciplines should be learning from them.

What about the other processes that general education is meant to teach, the ones that more clearly belong to the specific disciplines? Given the emphasis on process over content, we'd expect courses to be carefully planned to emphasize the process scientists use, the way historians think, and so on. But while the theory says professors are teaching process, which is why the particular content isn't important, how many plan their courses around this principle? Many schools allow science courses without labs to satisfy the general education requirement. Students in those courses don't get the opportunity to operate like a scientist, but merely to read about the results scientists have found. What about a history course? Are general education students assigned projects to dig through historical documents and data and write up their results, and then are they graded for their capability with that process? A similar point can be made for other subjects. Perhaps it could be claimed that process is present inevitably and students absorb it – it's in the air, can't be avoided. But that justification is a stretch. Students may be learning an obscure set of facts without ever coming to understand or appreciate the way of thinking within the discipline that houses them. So the claim to be teaching process can become an excuse for professors to teach whatever specialized courses they like. While process may be important for the curriculum designers among them who sit on committees and give a public face to the program of study, other professors, who do most of the teaching, may take process lightly.

Still, this is only one problem related to the process/content distinction – that schools are failing to live up to their billing in teaching important intellectual processes, whether it's the cross-disciplinary one of writing or a more discipline-specific one like historical analysis. The other problem of major proportion is the failure to recognize that beyond teaching process, the curriculum should put more emphasis on content. The notion that any particular content that works to teach a given process is okay – is a foolhardy notion. Relativism shows through again here. It isn't a full-blown relativism, since there is a knowledge claimed to be of greatest worth – process knowledge. But within the range of content, seemingly anything goes that can be geared toward teaching process. Where students lose out is that if they take a history course devoted to China or the Caribbean or American cinema to fulfill a general education requirement, they'll be learning content that holds much less importance for the practical aspects of their lives than if they took an American history survey. While they can learn about how historians think from any of those courses, it's more important in terms of a core of knowledge that they learn about the political party system in the U.S., our involvement in major wars, our immigration patterns and policies, and the give-and-take of big business versus labor unions than it is to know about the accomplishments of the Ming dynasty or the conflicts of Hispaniola or the innovations of Orson Welles and Stephen Spielberg. They need the former more than the latter in order to achieve adequate cultural literacy so they're well prepared for a wide range of situations they'll confront in their lives. Likewise in the sciences, if students satisfy their general education requirement by learning about the scientific method in a specialized course on human sexuality or on the solar system, they'll be missing out on the broader content they could have gotten in a general biology course or general physics course – content that's more applicable to our overall health and consciousness of our living environment than merely knowing about the reproductive process, or more applicable to understanding the basis behind all of the sciences, including the complicated electronic and nuclear world we live in.

What's at stake here is the very notion of "general" education. When what makes it general is conceived only in terms of process, and not content, the learning students get will be a patchwork of specialized parcels of information from here and there rather than a broad vision of the most significant basics available in each of the main areas of knowledge. Emphasis on process over content grossly distorts what it means to be broadly or liberally educated.

THE KNOWLEDGE EXPLOSION

Not all faculty, of course, buy into the process-knowledge rationale. There are firm believers in teaching broad content that's more important for students to have than narrow content. Those faculty still face a further challenge – about the sheer enormity of what's available to teach today, made so by the explosion of knowledge during the 20th century and continuing into the 21st century at a seemingly ever-accelerating rate. There is much more material now than there was a century ago when the idea of teaching survey courses in the various disciplines came into vogue. The challengers say professors in our time can't come close to teaching all of the important material, and they'll do better not to try. But the situation doesn't call for alarm. Two corollaries are attached to the pronouncement about the knowledge explosion that explain why missing the broad content of a survey approach to general education isn't a disturbing liability. One says that if students don't learn something, they can always look it up. We live in a computer age where access to information is much greater and quicker than in the past, and with advancements in technology, it will be even more so as time moves on. Knowledge is readily available to us at our fingertips. The other corollary says that new knowledge is generally better than old, and we should concentrate on what's new.

Knowledge is progressive – the old spawns the new, which then supersedes it. If students concentrate on what's new, they'll be getting the best that can be offered.

While these appeals to be updated and futuristic include just enough truth to be tempting, they constitute a jumble of confused thinking. What our confrontation with the knowledge explosion should tell us is not that we should give up attempting broad coverage of the most important points, but that now it's more imperative than ever that students get broad coverage. If knowledge is expanding in a way that makes navigating through it more and more difficult, then it's critical to be able to recognize the guideposts. Rather than less focus on survey knowledge, more focus is needed. We may have to be especially attentive in choosing what to include and what to leave out. But that's a challenge to be met rather than an excuse to give up.

Looking up whatever knowledge is missing is a simplistic answer. It's true that computers have made acquiring knowledge much easier and quicker than in the past. And in the last few years they've been miniaturized to be held in the palm of a hand, giving the source of immense intellectual storage the portability to go anywhere. In the 21st century people don't need to be sitting at a desk to look things up – they can learn on the go, at any time. But while it may seem that instant answers are the wave of the future, there are several reasons why this approach can't replace a solid education in the liberal arts.

Even if what someone looks up is available quickly, it doesn't help when it's needed immediately – in the middle of a business meeting or project where you're expected to be knowledgeable already and successful performance counts on it, or in a casual conversation where it's embarrassing to admit ignorance. And what happens when you're reading something that contains several or many puzzling references? Looking them all up, even if each one goes quickly, accumulates into considerable lost time.

Further, trying to comprehend the whole, you get bogged down in processing so much new knowledge.

But what if there is time? You're not hurried. Where do you start? What do you look for? Searching for a fact such as a date when an event occurred, or the definition of a word, might not take long, but sophisticated words are likely to involve cross-referencing. Statistics may be elusive, calling for more of a hunt. Broad concepts can prove more confounding yet. To look something up you need some basic knowledge to start with. The more you know about what you're looking for, the better equipped you are to find it. Querying a search engine requires you to know what key words to use, and sifting through the hundreds to millions of responses that may come up demands a sense of direction to cut through to the main objective. It's easier to fill in the blanks of knowledge if you already have some of the related blanks filled in, as with a crossword puzzle. Or to try another metaphor, just as in the world of finance it takes money to make money, in the world of the intellect it takes knowledge to gain knowledge. Someone who has the basics is in good shape to move on to more complicated matters. Someone without the basics will struggle to come up with the pieces by looking them up.

All of this has to do with information gathering in reaction to the discovery that something is missing. But acquiring a piece of information that's missing is having knowledge only on a surface level. Filling in a blank is being reactive, which is different than being proactive and applying acquired knowledge to new situations. For that, more understanding is needed, at least in many cases. The earlier list of content knowledge provides some examples. The term "postmodernism" is popular today, but making sense of it is difficult. Looking it up reveals the obvious, that it comes after modernism, but what is modernism? And there seems to be a political bent, but that's vague too. The term can be applied in many areas of the arts and sciences, and somehow in management theory. Before you're confident about discussing it in a business report, or even tossing it out in an impromptu discussion, you need to do more than consult a reference source for a definition.

Legal concepts and literary terms also can be puzzlers. Looking up the 14th Amendment tells us that it guarantees "due process of law" and "equal protection of the laws." What does that mean? How about the expression "begging the question?" Many reference sources give only a logician's explanation, confusing people by failing to note that the way the term is used more typically today, especially in journalism, is far different. "Quixotic" might seem easy enough to look up, but a brief dictionary definition can leave readers pondering – "extravagantly chivalrous or romantically idealist; visionary; impractical or impracticable." Does the word mean any of these things individually, or all of them together, or a limited combination? The dictionary also says the derivation is from Don Quixote, but unless you understand the personality of Cervantes' famous character, you won't be ready to use the word yourself.

Just as misleading as reliance on "looking it up" is the notion that new knowledge is better than old. In fact, most of what's new today will end up on the back shelf in the future, the same way most contemporary music will seldom be heard after its brief period of success. It's a mistake to assume that because something is recent it holds more worth than something that isn't. The sort of knowledge associated with the humanities makes this point well. It would be sheer hubris to think that the insights of Plato, Shakespeare, Machiavelli, and Dostoevsky have been overridden or reduced by the latest authors found in bookstores today, and that lessons learned from the Roman Empire, the Inquisition, the American Revolution, and the Impressionist movement in art have less to tell us than the latest political, religious, and cultural events and movements. The humanities in any era – new, old, or in between –

speak to the human condition, revealing our nature and tendencies, our triumphs and tragedies. Each era has its few geniuses and its events that stand out. With the passage of time they don't lose significance, but instead continue to put our minds in touch with the inner recesses of our being, just as they did the minds of our ancestors. Only a small amount of what may now seem relevant because it's contemporary will continue to seem that way for more than a decade or two, and then only a small amount of what continues at that point will eventually remain as having enduring value.

If that's the case for the humanities, what about the sciences? We're often told that science and the humanities are fundamentally different, and that even if it's conceded that the humanities are timeless, scientific knowledge is not. In science the latest really is best and it does supersede what came before it. We don't treat the thinking of the ancient world or the Renaissance or even a hundred years ago as instructive today. What we know now about the genome surpasses what Mendel dreamed of in the late 19th century. Our current understanding of atomic structure goes far beyond the path-breaking genius Bohr and Heisenberg were recognized for in the early 20th century. And what Mendel and Bohr and Heisenberg had to say in their day was far advanced over the science that came before it.

The path of science is progressive. Put in terms from the philosophy of science, scientific knowledge is cumulative and eliminative – it grows by consuming and building on what precedes it and discarding the unnecessary remains. Doesn't it make sense, then, when teaching science, to concentrate on the newest? Yes, but in a qualified way. The newest includes the aggregate of all from the past that's still considered viable, along with what's recently replaced the knowledge which is no longer considered to be part of the aggregate. The basics of biology and physics still include much that predates the work scientists are doing presently.

We have available to us today huge amounts of newly produced scientific material, but the explosion consists of various theories and statistical studies that often contradict one another, and most of which will be discarded before long. This material may be worthy of mention, but it doesn't belong as the mainstay of instruction in science, which should consist chiefly of the latest version of the aggregate. In science newer may be better, but when it comes to curriculum design for basic college study, that principle should be tempered by an emphasis on what has managed to stand the test of time.

A further caution here is that an interest in what's new shouldn't be taken as a reason to specialize at the expense of broad-based knowledge. Learning the basics of biology – whatever the contemporary version of the basics is – is more important than taking a course on innovations in genetics. Studying the foundations of physics – what's recognized today as the overall key content – is more valuable than focusing on innovative findings about our solar system. The fact that content is new, even the most brilliant and intriguing of the new, does no more than to say it should find a place amidst much other content. It doesn't belong as a stand-in for that other content. Science in general education can be up to date without ceding away the purpose of being general.

Let Common Sense Prevail

The knowledge explosion joins the process/content distinction in explaining why students can do without broad, survey knowledge. Both ideas begin with sensible observations that end up being twisted into faulty reasoning. It's clear that knowledge has grown to enormous proportions, and that a conceptual distinction can be made between process and content. But an overabundance of something doesn't mean we shouldn't or can't sort out the best of it, or that we can rely on technology to tap into what we need when we need it, or that all that's necessary is to skim off the latest and disregard the rest. And separating knowledge into two parts doesn't mean one of the parts is unimportant and accounting for it is unnecessary. What's assumed to be clever thinking about weighing and parsing knowledge misses the mark when it's applied to support a loosely structured curriculum.

Politics and relativism carry mistaken cleverness further. Beyond excusing the loss of comprehensive learning, they militate against its existence. The politics of diversity, while good for students in a moderate dose, is often promoted beyond its practical value and its standing in the grand scheme of knowledge. As a result, at many schools diversity has usurped valuable space in general education. Politicization has been spurred on by relativism, which demands opening the curriculum to nontraditional ways of thinking. Openness provides justification for the creation of a variety of unusual and specialized courses. It might seem this perspective would oppose playing favorites, including the buildup of diversity politics, but the force of relativism works in another way – to ward off diversity's critics by denying that they have a high ground of surpassing knowledge to back them up.

These four ideas – relativism, politics, process over content, and the knowledge explosion – dominate in a mindset that prefers the smorgasbord approach when studying the liberal arts. The term "general education" is still used to describe that approach, but today the meaning has loosened to become whatever collection of courses a student happens to take before settling into a major. What it doesn't mean is a comprehensive and coherent overview of the important elements of knowledge students should be acquainted with to be competent thinkers and to understand our world. General doesn't imply comprehensive, simply the sum of a few specialized parts. And it doesn't imply coherent – the result is random.

If general education in its present form is incoherent, the sensible answer is to redesign it. The faulty principles that support the smorgasbord model can be reversed to form the basis for a better way. Instead of relativism, a respect for hierarchy should prevail. Rather than letting students sample here and there as they like with an unhealthy result, colleges should admit that some knowledge is more important than other knowledge, and some is most important. It's the most important that should be found in general education, with everything else set aside for electives or for majors. When faculty object to this, they should be reminded that the purpose of basic liberal arts study isn't to give them an outlet to teach their specializations or a platform for whatever particular views they personally hold dear. It's to give students what they need, which means the foundational ideas of the culture they'll be living in. Diversity, although a part of that, answers to something larger. The principle of unity is more important – the unity of human nature as well as of the United States and its way of life and its roots in European culture.

Respect for hierarchy will tell us that separating process from content doesn't give license to downplay the significance of the content students are taught. Since teaching process doesn't require any particular content, it shouldn't be hard to ensure that when the proper content is identified, process isn't left out. The process of historians, for instance, isn't lost when the history of the U.S. and of Western Civilization are designated as of highest importance for the curriculum and other histories are not. And hierarchy speaks to the knowledge explosion, too, telling us that it's crucial not to give up in the face of the expansive amount of learning that's available – some of it is much more valuable than the rest. Knowing this produces confidence to forge on and identify what ought to be taught.

Once the excuse of relativism has been put aside, the rest of the faulty epistemology of general education follows. The replacement principles of hierarchy and unity lead in a different direction – toward a core curriculum. That means a carefully prescribed set of liberal arts courses all students take that provide a broad knowledge about history, literature, and philosophy, the techniques and history of the arts, the fundamental method and ideas underlying natural science along with the staple findings of its main divisions, likewise for the social sciences, and in math the rudiments of statistics and calculus along with a familiarity with computers. A solid program like this will take more than the minimum some schools today require of a single year's worth of general education. It might extend up to two years, with a shorter version for students in technical fields that have extensive requirements for professional certification. In sum, there will be several courses worth of learning for each of the main divisions of liberal arts knowledge (perhaps a little heavier on the humanities and sciences and a little lighter on the arts and math). The main idea is to emphasize the basics and not pretend that courses on specialized topics taught at the entry level can fill the bill. The aim is to give students an overall breadth of knowledge that includes a reasonable amount of depth as well, but not to force depth to an unneeded extent in any one area.

The specifics of what material is taught from each of the divisions of knowledge can be argued out at individual schools, but the expectation is that if faculty are being honest about what lies at the bedrock of their disciplines, rather than letting their personal preferences get the best of them, they will come up with reasonably similar accounts from one school to the next of what that is. With the key knowledge identified, it can be taught in standard courses like American Government, Introduction to Psychology, and so on, or it might be fashioned into an interdisciplinary format. Diversity might be handled in a single course, or perhaps as parts of several. Process can be monitored to see that the ways of thinking and the methods of the various disciplines are planned for. And with the cross-disciplinary process of writing, a core lends itself to careful coordination so that students not only get enough of it but they get different kinds. Research papers, argumentative essays, creative expression, project reports, lab reports, and perhaps even memos and letters can be built into the required courses, with the assurance that all students get full exposure.

Is a core curriculum model for our nation's colleges a real possibility? Or is the idea mere pie in the sky? It's not new, but the vast majority of schools haven't adopted it. What would it take to move them? There are faculty who will embrace a core, but many others who will cling to self-serving motives and faulty ideas about the nature of knowledge. Administrators and trustees will have to exercise control and set things straight. They may be intimidated by faculty claims to have intellectual authority and academic freedom, and by a lack of agreement among professors about what knowledge they favor. But the overseers have common sense behind them. They don't have to be history professors to know that in general education, U.S. history is very important while the history of the Caribbean trails far behind. They don't need to be biology professors to see that general biology is more important than a specialized course on marine biology. The same goes for other basic courses. It's not difficult to recognize a curriculum of quality compared with one that's substandard. The key question college leaders have to ask is whether their allegiance is more strongly toward pleasing their workers – or – to putting out the best product.

The other main concern they'll have about adopting a core is that their clientele may not buy it. Students often fail to recognize its value, especially since colleges demean general education by structuring it as a smorgasbord. They want to get through the preliminaries of their degree in the easiest way possible. Will those students avoid a college that has a solid set of basic curriculum requirements, and instead choose one where they can wander through an exotic menu of courses? Some will, probably many. But a school with a core will attract serious students, and serious students tend to be strong students. The college's academic profile may rise. What's given up in the quantity of people applying may be balanced by an increase in the quality of those who attend. And it may be that quantity isn't given up after all. A college dedicated to teaching a core could make quite a splash if it promoted its curriculum aggressively by publicizing why it's better than what other schools have – calling them out in open debate, naming prominent schools or groups of schools that promote the inferior standard of smorgasbord learning.

The crucial point to be made is how possession of core knowledge is in students' best interest – not simply the fact that it is, but how it is. The primary reason most students have for going to college is to prepare for the practical aspect of their lives ahead, especially for jobs. This is why they're investing their time and taking out loans. They need to be apprised of the ways a content-oriented core of liberal arts courses serves their goal. When college applicants consider what they'll be studying, they'll take notice of a pitch that differs from the standard emphasis on having lots of choice in the first year or two, one that instead spells out specifically the items of knowledge – not only skills but especially content found in a core approach to general education – that align with what they want from higher learning. A smorgasbord filled with tidbits of specialized information comes out the loser in a comparison. This lacking can be made clear by presenting examples of people who are shy on core knowledge and as a result flounder in perusing a report, listening to a presentation, assessing the claims of anyone from sales personnel to school officials to politicians, and even reading an editorial and talking with a co-worker or friend.

Getting quotable statements from employers and graduate schools can add cachet to this strategy. It reinforces the introduction of a seldom used maneuver into the competition to impress higher education's consumers. Trying to sell students on the liberal arts may seem odd in a climate where the worth of college studies is measured in utilitarian terms, but it makes sense for a school where the general education program is of a kind that fits those terms. And if one institution or a few can pull this off, others will be challenged to follow. If students can be made to see the practical advantage of a core curriculum, they may vote with their feet for a school that has one, so that market principles push college leaders to do what they've been unwilling to do otherwise.

– 8 –

LIBERAL LEARNING NEEDS A NEW P-R CAMPAIGN

It's no secret that college students and college graduates are lacking in basic liberal arts knowledge. Education policy analysts have long bemoaned the situation. Business leaders sometimes notice it too and complain about it. Surveys done every few years for various education organizations have highlighted the widespread ignorance. A 1989 Gallup survey of college seniors nationwide showed that slightly more than half knew when the Civil War occurred (in a 50-year span), what the Reconstruction period was, and that the Koran is the sacred text of Islam. Fewer than half knew what the Magna Carta was, what the Missouri Compromise decided, that the Mayans lived in Mexico, that the purpose of the *Federalist Papers* was to gain ratification of the U.S. Constitution, who wrote *The Tempest, The Republic,* or *Crime and Punishment,* and a raft of other information.

An earlier version of this of this essay appeared in *The Midwest Quarterly* 41 (1999), pp.88-116.

Another national survey of college seniors done by Roper in 1996 produced a worse picture. While Gallup used mostly multiple-choice questions (with a 25 percent chance of being correct from random guessing), this time respondents were required to fill in the blanks. Forty-seven percent knew how many U.S. senators there are, 8 percent knew that the expression "government of the people, by the people, for the people" comes from Lincoln's Gettysburg Address, 41 percent could name four major religions outside of Christianity, 24 percent could name four countries (any four) in Africa, 53 percent could figure out the perimeter of a room 65 feet wide and 35 feet long, 61 percent could compute how long it would take an airplane flying 6 miles a minute to travel 720 miles. The rest of the 20-question test was of a comparable level of difficulty. Only 7 percent of respondents answered 15 questions correctly, 70 percent failed to get half right, and a third scored on 5 or fewer.

More unflattering data came in a Roper survey of historical literacy done in 2000 at the top 55 colleges and universities in the nation (as named by *U.S. News*). Answering multiple-choice questions, just over half of our best and brightest could identify the Magna Carta, while slightly more than six in ten were aware of the purpose of the Monroe Doctrine and that the division of powers between the states and federal government is established in the Constitution. Fewer than 30 percent knew the meaning of Reconstruction, and the source of Lincoln's "government of the people..." phrase. In all, four out of five students graded a D or F on a test composed of questions drawn from a basic high school curriculum.

So much for an elite college education. We may expect students from elite schools to have a better basic knowledge than other students, but it still is embarrassingly weak. Just how much basic learning, then, do colleges provide? In 2006 and 2007 Roper surveyed freshmen and seniors at 50 institutions with 60 multiple-choice questions on civic literacy. Again ignorance abounded, as the respondents stumbled over the century when the first American colony was established, the meaning or significance of the *Federalist Papers*, indirect democracy, NATO, Roe v. Wade, inflation, the law of demand, and so on. Some of the questions were tough or tricky, but random guessing could earn 20 percent. The upshot, beyond reinforcing a picture of benightedness, lay in the overall scores of 52 percent (2006) and 51 percent (2007) for freshmen and 53 percent and 54 percent for seniors, showing that college had added nothing to their knowledge of basic civics. Scores at elite colleges ranged in the 60s while for other schools they were 10 to 20 points lower, but only two schools showed a gain of more than 10 points for seniors over freshmen, and sixteen (mostly elites) actually recorded a decline.

These surveys and others like them drive home the point about the basic learning that supposedly well-educated young Americans do not possess. How have our colleges dealt with the situation? What they haven't done is step up and overhaul the curriculum to ensure that students learn what the surveys show is lacking. For several decades many faculty and administrators have talked up the liberal arts portion of a college degree that goes by the name "general education," and busily and proudly gone about creating "reform." But the changes they've made have had little impact on the issue at hand. Some of the changes have done nothing for it at all – like adding diversity requirements and freshman seminars. Other changes are meant to deal with the missing knowledge, but what they amount to is merely a bit of restraint on the smorgasbord of courses students can choose from to fulfill their basic requirements. For whatever colleges have done in the name of reform, they continue to graduate students bereft of the basics. While critics find this to be a cause for alarm and an embarrassment for American education, the majority of the higher education community goes along with it. The critics' protests go unheeded. No matter how hard they try – and they've tried hard time and again – they fail to get enough people worked up about the situation to do something about it. The fact is that the dominant mindset doesn't see the knowledge in question as being important.

Professors – the experts entrusted with designing the curriculum – have other priorities. They often selfishly prefer to teach specialty courses and call that general education, rather than take on the broad-based, foundational courses students need. And they endorse theories that downgrade the fundamental knowledge that's lacking. They hold that knowledge is relative and there is no body of knowledge that is of ultimate worth, or that diversity should supersede the American and Western traditions, or that it's more important to prepare students to be agents of social change than to concentrate on learning a set of facts. These ideas lead to teaching all sorts of things in the name of liberal learning rather than the basics students are missing. It's not that there are no professors who believe in teaching the basics, but that the dominant mindset holds the ones who do in check.

If that's where the faculty stand, what about their students? The way professors think about the curriculum is one thing, but the way the people paying to study with them think is something else. They aren't concerned about maximizing their professors' job satisfaction, and they're not devoted to clever epistemological constructions, although they do absorb the message that liberal learning can't be too significant if the faculty don't agree on its purpose or what courses it should include. Students have their own take on knowledge, and it's simple – they want to acquire the kind they see as relating closely to their own lives, that applies well in today's world and helps them get along in it. To sum it up under a single word, they want knowledge that is practical, and they think of it especially in job-related terms. They don't see basic literature, history, geography, and so on as filling the bill. What's learned there appears to be frivolous, the sort of thing that's good for playing *Trivial Pursuit* or *Jeopardy*, the currency of elitist mind-games. But what difference does it make in the real world of practical everyday affairs if a person doesn't know about the Civil War, or about Shakespeare, or exactly where some place is located on the map? This is the way many students' parents see it as well, and the same goes for the general public.

Here is the challenge that liberal learning must meet if it's ever to have a chance of gaining widespread support and the respect it deserves. The impetus won't come from the dominant faculty mindset, but a coalition of dissenters within academia and critics from outside can provide the voice that's needed. Pointing out missing knowledge, as the surveys do, is only a first step. A strong promotion needs to be mounted for why what's missing is a problem. And it needs to be made on grounds nonbelievers are willing to listen to. They see the value of a college education in utilitarian terms. Believers need to find a better way to deal with this crucial factor than they have so far. In short, the situation calls for a new type of public relations campaign.

The old campaign has consisted of two main sales pitches – one that's antagonistic to the cause, and another that's been made only vaguely and without the force that could make it work. Oftentimes liberal learning has been presented as the antithesis of utilitarianism. Its value, we're told, is intrinsic. The pursuit is simply for its own sake. The gain is in the enrichment of the mind or soul. Activity done for its own sake is a higher form of activity than the practical, and something everyone who is initiated into it in college will benefit from. There have been many eloquent pronouncements to this effect, and in fact the idea is sound. It stands as an admirable reason for liberal learning. The problem is that it doesn't tell all of the story, and certainly not the story the utilitarian mindset is willing to listen to. It rubs the wrong way. For one thing, utilitarians who listen long enough to understand it want to know why students should spend their time and money in college on pursuits of intrinsic value, when what they're looking for is strictly practical. Many times, though, philosophical subtlety gets lost, and the devastating caricature comes out that portrays liberal learning as trivia. When this happens, no amount of moralizing about intrinsic worth is going to change people's minds. In either event, what they need to hear is the other part of the story about the worth of what they're rejecting. Learning the basics of the liberal arts is indeed practical. Studying them yields valuable knowledge of a utilitarian sort.

Advocates for liberal learning have raised this point, making it their other sales pitch. Many have conceded that the knowledge-for-its-own-sake position attracts few new followers, and they've taken to promoting the liberal arts as having an important practical dimension. But their explanations are brief and largely uninformative. Sometimes they seem to assume the answer is intuitively clear, and other times we get murky warnings about how a lack of basic liberal learning leads to failure to perform on the job or to our country being in a precarious position in the global marketplace. But generalizations like these don't get to the heart of the matter. What would do it are clear-cut examples of how having a broad liberal-arts knowledge prepares people to function well, and how lacking that knowledge leaves them ill-equipped. The challenge is to demonstrate specifically the way the knowledge in question applies in their own individual practical affairs – how it benefits them in a variety of situations they face in their everyday lives. And to show only a few situations won't be enough. The support that's essential for liberal learning lies in the cumulative effect of numerous examples of everyday occurrences. If it can be demonstrated that time and again knowing the basics of the liberal arts has true utilitarian value, the case will be strengthened for pushing colleges to ensure that their graduates have this sort of learning, and for convincing consumers of higher education that the effort to acquire it isn't foreign to their interests but actually consistent with them.

A good starting point in demonstrating the practicality of liberal learning lies in the concept of "cultural literacy." Its popularizer, E.D. Hirsch, in his book by that title, concentrates on the knowledge he believes students should acquire in high school, but it can be argued that much of the material he wants covered should also be found in the college curriculum. While this might seem like repetition, there are good reasons for it. One is that while students may be getting the important material at the secondary level (it may be suspected that many are not), obviously they haven't learned it or they wouldn't be showing their ignorance the way have on the surveys. The other reason is that, at the college level, courses deal with topics in a deeper and more sophisticated fashion. Important material gets a fully adult treatment.

The main point of cultural literacy is that human thinking and communication rely on the possession of a body of relevant background information. In order to pick up a newspaper or magazine or book and comprehend what it says, or do likewise in listening to someone speak, and particularly to think critically about and evaluate all of this – here another popular concept, "critical thinking," fits together with cultural literacy – a person must have knowledge of certain fundamental facts and ideas that come in the form of terms, dates, names. Otherwise there are many gaps in meaning, and understanding is reduced, along with the power to relate one thing to another and thereby make judgments. There is relevant prior knowledge we have to possess before what we read and hear makes sense to us and can be applied to understand our world and live in it well. Without this knowledge we can only stumble along.

Applying the notion of cultural literacy, taken at a level fitting among college graduates, it's possible to come up with examples of its importance in everyday life. These examples are hypothetical but realistic, and are meant to show that the instances where having cultural literacy makes a difference occur in many settings.

- During a job interview you're told that the firm's most successful people have Machiavellian tendencies. Just what is it that they value? In your last interview they were big on family values. Should you emphasize that?
- You read a summary of a movie that says about the main character, "He meets his Lady Macbeth." Perhaps you recognize the reference to a Shakespearean figure, or at least a famous figure from somewhere in literature. But what was she like?
- At an auction you consider buying a chair said to come from an important old southern family. "How old is it?," you ask. "Antebellum," you're told. "What's that mean?," you venture. The auctioneer smiles and answers mockingly, "Before the flood." Now wondering if the furniture in the room may be water-damaged, you examine the chair. On the underside there is a faded but readable manufacturer's seal dated 1894. Should you bid on the chair?
- You read in an editorial that a politician you're thinking of voting for has a strong superego. You assume that means he thinks too highly of himself.
- Holding an alphabetized client list, your boss sits down with you. She wants to go over it now to determine which clients to concentrate on. Those east of the Mississippi get a degree of preference. Your geographical sense can handle east coast and west coast, but the large mass of states in between is a mental blur. You're thinking of pulling up a map on your iPhone, but if the boss sees you don't know the basics about your company's business, you may lose points in your quest for a promotion.

- At a dinner party you're caught in a discussion about great landscape painters. Constable and Monet have been mentioned. The only famous artists who come to mind are Rembrandt and Picasso. Should you drop a name?

- At a meeting to explain the new marketing strategy for one of your company's feature products, your boss says that, "Americans aren't really Epicureans," but "we are into conspicuous consumption." You spend an uncomfortable half-hour nodding silently, trying to understand the logic of the new rationale and at the same time keep up with other things being said.

- You inquire about the academic performance of the students at the school where your child attends the fourth grade. You're given a sheet of information from standardized testing, with lots of numbers, and terms like "mean," "media," and "standard deviation." For the main test the school relies on, you see that the fourth graders have a mean percentile of 70 and a median percentile of 52. Are the fourth graders considerably above the national average, as the principal has announced?

- You ask what sort of mood someone is in, and you're told, "A docile 7.5 on the Richter scale." You wonder, "Is that a good mood or bad?" "If only I'd taken that Intro to Psychology course..."

- Your 7-year-old daughter sees a TV clip about a typhoon and asks if that's like the storm in *The Wizard of Oz*. "Sure," you reply, "a big storm," figuring that's a safe statement, and hoping there won't be a follow-up question.

- You read a business analysis that mentions "ad valorem," Keynesian," "invisible hand," and "economies of scale." The terms aren't entirely new, but you've always been fuzzy on economics lingo. You stumble along with the author's gist, but feel like your European friend who watches baseball occasionally but doesn't really get it.

Cultural literacy is practical, as these examples demonstrate. And there are many more – hundreds, at least – of key terms, dates, names that being familiar with is not a trivia exercise. Knowing them gives a person mobility of word and thought, a grasp of what's happening in the surrounding world that allows for successful navigation through it. Not knowing them means going through life encountering frequent confusions and uncertainties about what to do and say. In the absence of knowledge like this people may find ways to cope and get along, but in order to function at a high level in the world we live in, that knowledge is a prerequisite.

Still, as valuable as cultural literacy is, it explains only part of the worth of a solid liberal arts education. There's much more that holds importance. Beyond coming to know individual pieces of information is the capacity to put the pieces together so as to see the big picture. Education critic Jacques Barzun has referred to this kind of thinking as "general intelligence." The reference isn't to native capacity, or what might be called IQ, but instead to the trained capacity to make sense out of or give structure to the many and diverse ideas and facts floating around in our lives. General intelligence allows people to go beyond a single mindset or single discipline, beyond limited and narrow perspectives on the world.

More specifically, what's involved includes the ability to analyze or sort out information and to synthesize it and generalize, and beyond that, to prioritize and evaluate it. The process of doing all of this requires not only a great deal of factual knowledge, but an understanding of certain fundamental ideas that underlie the various disciplines and all high-level intellectualization. Accomplished thinkers eventually come to apply these ideas comfortably, by understanding what their components are and how the ideas fit together with one another. Overall there is an emphasis on understanding humanity and understanding how human beings fit into the larger scheme of things – what that scheme consists of, what we can control and what we can't, and to what extent.

This is general intelligence in the abstract. To put it in more concrete terms, naming some of the ideas will help, with a closer look at a couple of them to see just how they're involved in practical everyday affairs. As with cultural literacy, some examples should spell things out. Philosopher Mortimer Adler has identified 102 "Great Ideas," each divided into topics and some into subtopics, that underlie the structure of the Western intellectual tradition, the tradition of the society we live in. Adler's list is an excellent source for understanding what the fundamental ideas are, although there is easily room for debate about whether he was fully comprehensive and about which ideas are really the most fundamental and which belong as topics and subtopics. And while Adler prefers to aim only at the Western tradition, the fundamental nature of the ideas makes many of them applicable for other cultures as well.

Some examples from Adler's list include beauty, change, citizen, duty, eternity, family, freedom, God, induction, labor, love, mechanics, punishment, quantity, revolution, slavery, time, truth, war and peace, and will. These concepts are obviously fundamental, although some are more broad and extensive than others. They're much larger in scope than the typical items of cultural literacy, but the two types of knowledge aren't discrete. They overlap and converge, with general intelligence containing and organizing items of cultural literacy, and the recognition of those items drawing upon a comprehension of fundamental ideas.

The meaning of Sigmund Freud's term "superego," used in the earlier example about a politician, is a recognizable item of cultural literacy. The superego is one of the main elements in the picture Freud presents of the human psyche. But it's not this specific picture itself that is Freud's most significant contribution to our basic knowledge of things. That distinction goes to his positing of the unconscious mind – the notion that beneath the conscious level of the mind there lies another level, the unconscious, that influences it. The concept of the unconscious mind is a fundamental one, basic to psychology and discussed in philosophy, and sometimes drawn upon in other disciplines. (Adler's schema treats it as a sub-topic of the idea of mind.) Freud's identification of the unconscious was picked up by other theorists who offered their own versions of what its contents and workings are. In practical terms the idea of the unconscious translates into the recognition that what's inside people's minds as an influence on behavior often isn't clear or even available to their conscious understanding of themselves and the world. Based on this notion, various personality tests have been devised to reveal a person's inner self, and competing versions of the nature of the unconscious have led to competing approaches to therapy for mental illness.

For all of its influence though, Freud's psychodynamic approach to psychology isn't the only one. Other approaches have developed, and gained recognition for their own labels. In the cognitive approach the unconscious isn't denied, but emphasis is put on the processes of the conscious mind, and therapy follows suit. Humanistic psychology also emphasizes conscious thought but keys on existential or value choice, and in group settings links to sensitivity training. The behaviorist approach, in contrast, downplays the contents of people's minds and focuses on the actions they take. Various behavior modification strategies (rewards for desirable behavior, punishment for unacceptable behavior) have been devised to deal with problems of smoking, overeating, physical aggression, and so on.

Still, the idea of the unconscious mind is highly influential in our way of thinking. It explains what for many centuries had simply been called "madness," and thought of as inscrutable or deemed the work of Satan. We now have elaborate scientific explanations for mental illness, and the role of the unconscious is well accepted as the basis for them. The idea is important, too, in our understanding of criminality. Many legal cases involve defenses built around the idea of deep-seated psychological problems that are introduced as mitigating factors in judging criminal behavior. Further yet, we employ the notion of the unconscious in dealing with other important social problems – racism, for instance. The stage was set in the landmark Brown v. Board of Education case, where the decision to desegregate schools relied on the notion of psychological damage to young minds – that black children develop deep-seated feelings of inferiority by being isolated in segregated schools. Today the claim is heard that white people harbor underlying attitudes of racism they're not conscious of.

Given that the notion of the unconscious is a mainstay of 21st-century thought, how does it touch specifically on the lives of people who could benefit from having studied about it in college? As with cultural literacy, the challenge is to show how having a particular sort of knowledge in a person's background is an advantage in situations that person may encounter, in other words, how having that knowledge is valuable for more than arm-chair intellectualizing. There are various situations where what can be learned about the unconscious (and related matters like schools of psychology and psychological testing) through a good liberal arts education in college – the understanding about it that develops – will be helpful.

- A friend or member of your family has psychological problems. You want to help in choosing a professional for the person to see. You get advice and referrals, but are confused by the various professional titles of psychiatrist, psychologist, counselor, psychotherapist, social worker, and even more so by terms like "behavior modification," "gestalt," and "transactional analysis." Maybe all of this is just a sign of hyper-specialization, you think, and you simply need to pick someone with a good record. But if you were looking for advice on politics, wouldn't you consider the differences among Republican, Democrat, Libertarian, and Socialist? Or for cancer treatment among surgery, radiology, homeopathy, and gene therapy?

- You're on a jury where a psychological profile is part of the defense's case. A fellow juror says, "That's all Freudian baloney. You're responsible for your actions, period." Where do you stand?

- The company you work for in a managerial role is trying to deal with problems of absenteeism and theft among the employees. You have a voice in deciding what should be done. Should personality testing be used to screen employees or potential employees? Should you hire counseling psychologists to deal with offenders or potential offenders? Should you take the general preventive measure of having all employees go through a "consciousness raising" program? Should you consider behavior modification techniques? Are you better off simply hiring a better security force, maybe including undercover detectives?

- As a member of a union you are presented with a wage and benefits proposal to vote on. One controversial item is whether or not to include psychiatric/psychological services among the medical benefits – which will cost more. Where do you stand?

- In a salary discussion with your boss, you're asked why you are entitled to a raise when your performance has been judged average and not exemplary. You are a member of a minority group, but can't cite overt instances of racism against you. Do you want to introduce the topic of racist "tendencies?"

Having learned in college about the unconscious mind, and related matters in psychology, won't mean that someone can answer these questions easily. There are legal, ethical, and economic factors to be taken into consideration as well. And the psychological factors are not clear-cut – they involve opinions and value judgments. But a basic understanding of fundamental ideas is important for making the opinions and value judgments to be informed ones. People who have a working knowledge of the fundamental ideas that underlie or subsume the rest of our thinking, the ideas that inform us when we make difficult choices, are more ready than other people to make those choices and to do it well.

As another example of a fundamental idea, consider the idea of freedom. This idea underlies many issues we hold opinions about, and situations we confront. Our preference for a political party is likely to be determined by the extent to which and ways in which we believe government should exert control in our lives. Matters like gun control, abortion, free market economy, affirmative action, immigration, school prayer, and others we debate about and that are key factors in determining who we want to represent us in political office, involve the idea of freedom. And decisions made by legislators and judges about these issues directly affect everyday life – automobile manufacturers are forced to recall automobiles with questionable safety records, minority-owned businesses are given preference over white-owned businesses in securing government contracts, and so on. But the idea of freedom carries further into areas of everyday life that may not fall within the scope of our lawmakers and interpreters, and that don't make the national news. Yet here again, as with the high-visibility issues, having a well-thought-out understanding of what freedom is all about will be valuable.

- One of your coworkers likes to play rap music while on the job, within earshot of other workers who complain. A discussion comes up about cultural insensitivity, objectionable content in rap, and constitutional rights. Should the music be stopped?
- You're told by the local merchant's association the the new sign you've put up advertising your business doesn't conform to the association's standards – because it's too large and brightly colored. Will you change your sign? Just what is at issue here?
- One of your neighbors asks for your signature on a petition to erase the ordinance in your state requiring motorcyclists to wear helmets. He's glad to discuss the issue with you. How do you approach it?
- The school district where your children are enrolled is considering requiring students to wear uniforms. Do you find this to be an abridgment of freedom? If so, is it an acceptable one?
- The school district where your children are enrolled is considering offering a Bible course. The proposal causes much debate over freedom of religion and separation of church and state. Where do you stand?
- You have a well-paying professional job where you're performing successfully. But you're tired of the rat race. You consider several options – yoga, quitting your job and becoming an at-home consultant via distance media, selling your property and moving to an inexpensive cottage. What should you do, and just what is this elusive freedom that you seek?

- A religious figure makes the statement that the many freedoms we have are actually limiting – ultimate freedom is to know God and to know truth. What does this mean?

Just as with the idea of the unconscious mind, having a well developed understanding of freedom doesn't mean you can come to easy answers when confronted with issues and situations that involve it. And people who haven't gone to college, as well as people who have but haven't learned much about the basics of the liberal arts, still employ the notion of freedom in their thinking, and still face the same kinds of issues and situations that more fully educated people do. How, then, does having a solid liberal education in college make a difference? One thing students should learn in college is a bit about our political system, particularly about the United States Constitution – what freedoms are granted under it, and what decisions were rendered in some of our most famous court cases. Moving on to the study of history we can learn of concrete instances in the quest for freedom that relate directly to our lives today and indirectly to our understanding of humanity in general – about wars and rebellions fought for freedom (the American Revolution, French Revolution, Russian Revolution, and lesser-scale revolts like the Whiskey Rebellion, Boxer Rebellion, Hungarian Revolution), about the migrations of people for the purpose of finding freedom, about the civil rights movement, the labor movement, and so on. And beyond history lies the subject matter of philosophy, economics, literature. In being exposed to insights found in works like *On Liberty*, *Common Sense*, *Wealth of Nations*, *The Social Contract*, *The Communist Manifesto*, *The Second Sex*, *Invisible Man*, *1984*, *The Brothers Karamazov*, the Bible, the Bhagavad Gita, the Upanishads, and more, students come to consider the origins of freedom as a natural right and as created by human law, the concept of equal rights, the tension between freedom and responsibility, limitations on freedom by race and gender, and distinctions among types of freedom such as freedom of expression, religion, economic being, thought, and the soul.

People who learn about the events of history, about the foundations of our system of law, and about fundamental philosophical considerations concerning freedom are better equipped than those who haven't gained this knowledge are to deal with issues and situations such as those described here. They're able to make informed decisions when a claim like "I've got my constitutional rights" affects them directly. They know what concepts such as "ultimate freedom" actually mean. They know how changes that have occurred in history come into play when judging if we've gone too far or not far enough in the quest for freedom (for instance, from emancipation from slavery to affirmative action). They've learned about our nation's tradition of church/state separation and what it means for our schools. They perceive that freedoms for one group sometimes conflict with those of another, and they can weigh those situations thoughtfully (such as in playing the music of your choice versus not having to listen to offensive messages).

The various examples cited here of cultural literacy and "general intelligence" demonstrate that basic liberal arts learning is far from the trivia exercise that its detractors portray. Knowing about Shakespeare, about where some place is located on the map, about the abstract concept of freedom, and so on does make a difference in a person's life. As the examples suggest, that difference can be understood in utilitarian terms. Liberal learning is practical – it can be applied in ways that make us more comfortable, more successful in dealing with many circumstances we encounter in our daily activities. One way comfort or success is thought of is in terms of the job world – not in job-specific terms like knowing the tensile strength of building materials in engineering, or in marketing knowing how to construct a particular type of advertisement for a particular occasion. Instead the knowledge that liberal learning provides is the sort that can be applied across a variety of occupations to deal with contexts that move outside the details of specialization. It's the sort of knowledge that extends a person beyond being a mere technician in any given field, and produces a more comprehensive competence. This knowledge includes the factual information and fundamental ideas necessary for understanding what intelligent, educated people have to say, for getting along with fellow workers, for making management decisions, for understanding someone's place and worth in the general scheme of things. These are not trivial matters. They're crucial ones that confront a person time and again on the job and that can spell success or failure there.

So far this describes how the knowledge in question contributes to the workplace, in terms that practical-minded critics of the liberal arts should be willing to listen to. But preparation for jobs isn't the only educational ideal that liberal learning serves. Many of the examples given here describe personal and civic situations rather than job-related ones. They're as much a part of our everyday lives as our jobs are, and they're practical in nature. Liberal arts knowledge helps us deal with them. Getting along with friends and neighbors, making wise choices for our children, and dealing with community issues that require our input – these are all areas of life where we need knowledge of a practical sort, knowledge that helps us to get things done and to accomplish goals. While it's not as common to think of college studies being valuable in this way as it is to think in vocational terms, the case is there to be made, and if it's made clearly, it will feature the utilitarian bent that's shared with preparing students for jobs.

Looking further at the overlap of the personal and civic realms with the vocational, we can see how it goes beyond the abstract and into specific examples. A conflict over rap music in the workplace might just as easily occur in a domestic setting. It could involve roommates or neighbors instead of coworkers. The example about motorcycle helmets could be recast in terms of wearing safety gear on the job. Terminology drawn from economics or politics or psychology could pop up at home or at work. The practical matters that liberal learning prepares people to deal with aren't compartmentalized to one aspect of life or another.

It's tempting to go further in discussing the philosophy of knowledge and human activity, and perhaps reintroduce the notion of the intrinsic worth of liberal learning that stands as an admirable educational ideal. Much more could be said. But it would be counter to the point. The philosophical generalities and lofty appeals have been heard before, and they're precisely what nonbelievers have found unconvincing. What's important – the component that's been missing from the promotion of the liberal arts and is needed to make it convincing – are specific examples of practical matters. The examples given here are a start. Surely there are many more that other people can cite – of everyday situations a typical college graduate might face where having basic liberal arts knowledge can spell the difference between success and failure, or awareness and confusion. If enough examples are brought to light and enough emphasis is placed on them, then people who dismiss liberal learning as trivia may begin to change their minds and see its true worth. This describes the kind of new P-R campaign that supporters of liberal learning need to mount. Their product is excellent, but the sales pitch they've been using has limited appeal. It's time to revise the pitch, to put it in terms that tell people more concretely and graphically about the qualities of the product that make it good for them.

NOTES

1. DOES COLLEGE COST TOO MUCH?

2 We find tuition to be: "Tuition and Fee and Room and Board Charges, 2010-11," Table A, College Board, http://trends.collegeboard.org/college_pricing/report_findings/indicator/accessible/Tuition_and_Fees_and_Room_Board_Charges_2010_11.

2 In 1980 the average tuition: Claudia Golden and Lawrence F. Katz, *The Race Between Education and Technology* (Cambridge, MA: Harvard University Press, 2008), pp. 276-77.

2 over the last three decades: "Measuring Up 2008: The National Report Card on Higher Education," National Center for Public Policy and Higher Education, http://measuringup2008.highereducation.org/print/NCPPHEMUNationalRpt.pdf, p.8.

2 Room and board hikes: Richard Vedder, *Going Broke by Degree: Why College Costs Too Much* (Washington, DC: American Enterprise Institute, 2004), p. 85.

3 In the mid-1990s: "2003-04 Quick Facts about Student Debt," The Project on Student Debt, http://projectonstudentdebt.org/files/pub//2003-04_quick_facts.pdf, May 2007.

3 The average amount owed at graduation: "Student Debt and the Class of 2010," The Project on Student Debt, http://projectonstudentdebt.org/files/pub/classof2010.pdf, p.1.

4 institutional grants go to the wealthiest students: "Measuring Up 2008."

5 bachelor's degree holders: "Median Earnings in the Past 12 Months (in 2007 Inflation-Adjusted Dollars) by Sex and Educational Attainment for the Population 25 Years and Over," U.S. Census Bureau, http://factfinder.census.gov/servlet/DTTable?_bm=y&-geo_id=0100US&-ds_name=ACS_2007_1YR_G2000_B20004&-format=&-CONTEXT=dt.

6 The cost there is rising: "Measuring Up 2008."

6 Colleges have expanded: "Fast Facts," National Center for Education Statistics, http://nces.ed.gov/fastfacts/display.asp?id=98.

9 Over the last three decades: "2007-2008 Report on the Economic Status of the Profession," American Association of University Professors, http://www.aaup.org/AAUP/comm/rep/Z/ecstatreport2007-08/survey2007-08.htm?PF=1, p. 7.

9 by less than one percent: "Don't Blame the Faculty: The Annual Report on the Economic Status of the Profession 2003-04," Table E, American Association of University Professors,www.aaup.org/NR/rydonlres/3217785D-DED5-40A9-B1A4-B902AC309774/0/04z.pdf.

10 In 1970 the average teaching load: "Faculty Load Policies and Practices in Colleges and Universities," National Education Association, http://www.eric.ed.gov/ERICWebPortal/recordDetail?accno=ED068029, July 1972.

10 including virtually all of the top 100: "Faculty Teaching Load at the Top 100 Liberal Arts Colleges with Semester System – 2007 (top 100 per US News and World Report)," http://academics.eckerd.edu/instructor/weppnesp/SCR/topschools.pdf.

14 in the past several years: David Leonhardt, "Money and College; What a Deal!," *New York Times*, http://query.nytimes.com/gst/fullpage.html?res=980CE0D71E38F933 A15757C0A96E9C8B63, April 20, 2008.

16 for the last decade: "Annual Reported Spending Rates for U.S. Higher Education Endowments and Affiliated Foundations, Fiscal Years 2000-2009," National Association of College and University Business Officers, http://nacubo. org/Documents/research/2009_NCSE_Public_Tables_Spending_Rates.pdf.

17 since roughly 60 schools: "Institutions Listed by Fiscal Year 2006 Market Value Endowment Assets with Percentage Change Between 2005 and 2006 Endowment Assets," National Association of College and University Business Officers, http://www.nacubo.org/documents/research/2006NEW_Listing.pdf.

18 some schools offer online: For example, at Northeastern University, Liberty University, the University of Texas, St. Leo University, and Bowling State University the online tuition price is substantially cheaper to slightly cheaper than for on-campus courses. At the University of Massachusetts, University of Louisville, University of Maryland, University of Illinois, University of North Carolina at Greensboro, Indian Hills Community College, and Eastern Washington University the cost is the same (or nearly so) for online and on-campus, while at the Community College of Denver, University of Montana, University of North Carolina at Chapel Hill, State University of New York four-year campuses, and Michigan Technological University online costs somewhat more.

18 large public institutions now encouraging: Examples are the University of Maryland system, University of Minnesota system, University of Florida, Univ of Iowa, and University of North Carolina at Chapel Hill. See Trip Gabriel, "Learning in Dorm, Because Class is on the Web," *New York Times*, www. nytimes.com/2010/11/05 college.html?_r=1. See also Marc Parry, "Tomorrow's College," *Chronicle of Higher Education*, http://chronicle.com/article/Tomorrows-College/125120/.

19 a few schools (MIT, Carnegie Mellon, Yale): http://.ocw.mit/OcwWeb/ web/home/home/index.htm; http://.oli.web.cmu.edu; http://oyc.yale.edu.

19 The MITx program: Marc Parry, "MITx Will Offer Certificates to Outside Students Who Take Its Online Offerings," *Chronicle of Higher Education*, December 19, 2011.

19 substantially fewer than half: Elaine Allen and Jeff Seaman, "Learning on Demand: Online Education in the United States, 2009," Babson Survey Research Group and the SloanCorporation, http://www.sloanc.org/publications/survey/pdf/learningondemand.pdf, January 2010.

2. RANKING COLLEGES

28 As the story goes: Nicholas Thompson, "Playing with Numbers: How *U.S. News* Mismeasures Higher Education and What to Do about It," *Washington Monthly*, September 2000.

29 A trick for improving: Steve Stecklow, "Cheat Sheets: Colleges Inflate SATs and Graduation Rates in Popular Guidebooks," *Wall Street Journal*, April 5, 1995.

30 Acceptance rate can be lowered: Alvin P. Sanoff, "The *U.S. News* College Ratings: A View from the Inside," in *College and University Ranking Systems: Global Perspectives and American Challenges* (Washington, DC: Institute for Higher Education Policy, April 2007), http://www.ihep.org/assets/files//publications/AF/CollegeRankingSystems.pdf.

41 A good model: See "What Will They Learn?: A Guide to What College Rankings Don't Tell You" at http://www.whatwilltheylearn.com, a project of the American Council of Trustees and Alumni (http://www.goacta.org).

45 Consider the backgrounds: Joseph Santo, "Where the Fortune 50 CEOs Went to College," *Time*, August 15, 2006.

45 Among our nation's governors: For information on governors, I consulted the 50 websites. For the Congress, see "Current Members of the United States Congress" at http://en.wikipedia.org/wiki/Current_members_of_the_United_States_Congress.

46 Over the duration of their careers: Stacey Berg Dale and Alan Krueger, "Estimating the Payoff to Attending a More Selective College: An Application of Selection on Observables and Unobservables," *Quarterly Journal of Economics* 117 (2002). Available online at http://www.irs.princeton.edu/pubs/pdfs/409revised.pfd. See also the same authors' followup study, "Estimating the Return to College Selectivity over the Career Using Administrative Earning Data," Working Paper #563, Princeton University Industrial Relations Section, February 2011.

46 A 2008 survey: The survey, titled, "Getting a Foot in the Door – What Entry-Level Employers Want Most," was done by collegegrad.com. A summary can be found at http://jobs.aol.com/articles/2009/10/02/getting-a-foot-in-the-door-what-entry-level-employers-want-most.

3. AFFIRMATIVE ACTION AND ELUSIVE EQUALITY

61 In the 1970s: The data comparing SAT scores for whites and minorities appear in "The Widening Racial Scoring Gap on the SAT College Admissions Test," *Journal of Blacks in Higher Education* (Autumn 2005), http://jbhe.com/features/49_college_admissions-test.html, February 28, 2006. See also, "Digest of Education Statistics: 2008, Table 143," National Center for Education Statistics, http://ncess.gov/programs/digest/d08/tables/dt08_141.asp?referrer=list.

61 The grades of minority students: William G. Bowen and Derek Bok, *The Shape of the River: Long-Term Consequences of Considering Race in College and University Admissions* (Princeton, NJ: Princeton University Press, 1998). See also, Thomas Espenshade and Alexandria Walston Radford, *No Longer Separate, Not Yet Equal: Race and Class in Elite College Admission and Campus Life* (Princeton, NJ: Princeton University Press, 2009).

61 minorities' test scores: The graduate admissions test-score data are drawn from the organizations that administer the exams. For the GRE, see "Factors that Can Influence Performance on the GRE General Test 2006-2007," Table C2, Educational Testing Service, www.ets.org/Media/Tests?GRE/pdfgre_0809_

factors_2006-07.pdf. For the GMAT, see "Profile of Graduate Management Admission Test Candidates 2004-2005 through 2008-2009," Table A, Graduate Management Admission Council, www.gmac.com/NR/rdonlyres/EEFE1A18-4FCE-421D-ACE1-67C9D86A444B/0/ProfileofGMATCandidates0509.pdf. For the MCAT, see "Table 19: MCAT Scores and GPAs for Applicants and Matriculants to U.S. Medical Schools by Race and Ethnicity, 2009," Association of American Medical Colleges: Data Warehouse: Applicant Matriculant File as of 10/14/2009, www.aamc.org/download/85998/data/table19mcatpgaraceeth09web.pdf. For the LSAT, see "LSAT Performance by Race/Ethnicity," Tablee 4, Law School Admission Council LSAT Technical Report 08-03 October 2008, www.lcas.org/LsacResources/Research/TR/TR-08-03.pdf

62 A provocative and comprehensive study: Richard H. Sander, "A Systematic Analysis of Affirmative Action in American Law Schools," *Stanford Law Review* 57 (November 2004).

64 Another major study: Stephen Cole and Elinor Barbor, *Increasing Faculty Diversity: The Occupational Choices of High-Achieving Minority Students* (Cambridge, MA: Harvard University Press, 2003).

65 Psychologists, sociologists, and other: See, for instance, John Agbu, *Black American Students in an Affluent School: A Study of Academic Disengagement* (Mahwah, NJ: Lawrence Earlbaum Associates, 2003); Shelby Steele, *The Content of Our Character: A New Vision of Race in America* (New York: St. Martin's Press, 1990); John McWhorter, *Losing the Race: Self-Sabotage in Black America* (New York: Free Press, 2000); Douglas Massey et al., *The Source of the River: The Social Origins of Freshmen at America's Selective Colleges and Universities* (Princeton, NJ: Princeton University Press, 2003); Claude M. Steele, "Thin Ice: Stereotype Threat and Black College Students," *Atlantic Monthly*, August 1992.

69 The argument is sometimes couched: *The Shape of the River*.

70 Data show that: See in this volume, "Ranking Colleges," p. 56, 229.

4. LEGACIES, FINANCE, AND FAIRNESS

80 legacies account for perhaps one in seven: Daniel Golden, "An Analytic Survey of Legacy Preference," in *Affirmative Action for the Rich: Legacy Preferences in College Admissions*, ed. Richard D. Kahlenberg (New York: Century Foundation, 2010), p. 75.

81 75 percent of the public opposes it: Jeffrey Selingo, "U.S. Public's Confidence in Colleges Remains High," *Chronicle of Higher Education*, May 7, 2004.

83 One study of three elite schools: Thomas J. Espenshade, Chang Y. Chung, and Joan L. Walling, *Social Science Quarterly* 85 (December 2004), p. 1431.

83 Another study of 30: Michael Hurwitz, "The Impact of Legacy Status on Undergraduate Admissions at Elite Colleges and Universities, *Economics of Education Review* (December 2010).

88 The highest level decision on record: *Rosenstock v. Board of Governors of the University of North Carolina* (1961), p. 7.

89 the often forgotten Nobility Clause: Carlton F.W. Larson, "Titles of Nobility, Hereditary Privilege, and the Unconstitutionality of Legacy Preferences in Public School Admissions," *Washington University Law Review* 84, no.6 (2006).

89 cites the Equal Protection Clause: Steve D. Shadowan, Sozi P. Tulante, and Shara L. Alpern, "No Distinctions Except Those Which Merit Originates: The Unlawfulnes of Legacy Preferences in Public and Private Institutions," *Santa Clara Law Review* 49 (2009).

90 65 percent of legacy parents: George Leef, "Legacy Admissions – Affirmative Action for the Rich?," John William Pope Center for Higher Education Policy, http://www.popecenter.org/issues/article.html?id=1966, February 19, 2008. The school reporting was the University of Virginia.

91 another single school traced: Jonathan Meer and Harvey S. Rosen, "Altruism and the Child-Care Cycle of Alumni Giving," National Bureau of Economic Research Working Parer 13152, June 2007.

92 A recent study says no: Chad Coffman, Tara O'Neil, and Brian Starr, "An Empirical Analysis of the Impact of Legacy Preferences on Alumni Giving at Top Universities," in *Affirmative Action for the Rich.*

95 against the federal tax code: This argument is explained well by Peter Saks in "The Political Economy of Legacy Admissions, Taxpayer Subsidies, and Excess 'Profits' in American Higher Education: Strategies for Reform," in *Affirmative Action for the Rich.*

96 a precedent already exists: Congress did this through the Solomon Amendment to the 1995 *Omnibus Consolidated Appropriations Act.*

96 upheld by the U.S. Supreme Court: *Rumsfeld v. Forum for Academic and Institutional Rights*, 04-1152 (2006).

5. BIG-TIME "AMATEUR" SPORTS

100 budgets of $100 million: "NCAA College Athletics Finance Database," http://www.usatoday.com/sports/college/ncaa-finances.htm.

101 half a million to a million: Pete Thamel, "In College Football, Big Paydays for Humiliation," *New York Times*, August 23, 2006.

101 Coaches contracts in football and basketball: "Compensation for Division I Men's Basketball Coaches," http://www.usatoday.com/sports/graphics/basketball_contracts/flash.htm; "College Football – Highest Paid Coaches," www.americasbestonline.net/index.php/pages/collegehighestpaidcoaches.html.

101 the total time they put into their sports: Brad Wolverton, "College Football Players Spend 44.8 Hours a Week on their Sport, NCAA Survey Finds," *Chronicle of Higher Education*, January 14, 2008.

109 nearly 95 percent of: "FBS Athletic Revenues and Expenses," *Beyond the Blue Disk*, National Collegiate Athletic Association, 2010.

110 A third of the schools: "Chart: Analyzing the Percentage of tuition that goes to Athletics," www.usatoday.com/sports/college/2010-09-21-athletic-fees-chart_N.htm.

110 Schools that might be tempted: "2011-12 NCAA Division I Manual," National Collegiate Athletic Association, www.ncaapublications.com/productdownloads/D112.pdf.

112 accounted for about 6 percent: "Jonathan Orszag and Mark Israel, "The Empirical Effects of Collegiate Athletics: An Update Based on 2004-2—7 Data," http://web1.ncaa.org/web_files/president_reports/2009%20Repeort.pdf.

113 average nearly 40 hours a week: "College Football Players Spend 44.8 Hours a Week on their Sport, NCAA Survey Finds."

118 dubbed the whole affair: Murray Sperber, *Beer and Circus: How Big-Time College Sports Is Crippling Undergraduate Education* (New York: Henry Holt, 2000).

6. COLLEGE GOES TO HIGH SCHOOL

128 Records of AP test-takers show: "Annual AP Program Participation 1956-2011," http://professionals.collegeboard.com/profdownload/AP-Annual-Participation.pdf.

129 It had become commonplace: "Access to Excellence," Commission on the Future of the Advanced Placement Program, 2001.

129 Dissatisfied that standard remedial efforts: Jay Mathews, "Is AP for All a Formula for Failure?," *Washington Post*, June 28, 2009.

130 On a 5-point scale: "AP Score Distributions – All Subjects 1991-2011," College Board, http://professionals.collegeboard.com/profdownload/AP-Score-Distribution-All-Subjects-2011.pdf.

131 There are significant studies: For instance, K. Klopfenstein and M.K. Thomas, "The Link Between Advanced Placement Experience and Early College Success," *Southern Economic Journal* 75 (January 2009); William Lichten, "Whither Advanced Placement?," *Education Policy and Analysis* 29 (June 24, 2000).

131 from the Harvard Science Education Department: Philip M. Sadler and Robert H. Tai, "Advanced Placement Exam Scores as a Predictor of Performance in Introductory College Biology, Chemistry, and Physics Courses," *Science Educator* 16 (Spring 2007).

133 answering half or fewer of the questions: Philip M. Sadler and Robert H. Tai, "Advanced Placement Exam Scores as a Predictor of Performance in Introductory Biology, Chemistry, and Physics Courses."

135 In a 2008 survey: "Growing Pains in the Advanced Placement Program: Do Tough Trade-Offs Lie Ahead?," Thomas B. Fordham Institute, www.eric.ed.gov/PDFS/ED505527.pdf., 2009.

135 By the College Board's own estimate: "Access to Excellence: A Report of the Commission on the Future of the Advanced Placement Program," College Entrance Examination Board, 2001.

140 At least several dozen respected schools: Independent Curriculum Group, www.independentcurriculumgroup.org.

7. QUADRUPLE WHAMMY ON THE CURRICULUM

145 80 percent according to a recent survey: "Trends and Emerging Practices in General Education," Hart Research Associates, May 2009. Conducted for the Association of American Colleges and Universities.

147 from national surveys: For surveys of cultural literacy, see in this volume, "Liberal Learning Needs a New PR Campaign," pp. 177-179. For surveys of basic skills, see Justin D. Baer, Andrea L. Cook, and Stephen Baldi, "The

Literacy of America's College Students," American Institutes for Research, 2006 (commissioned by the Pew Charitable Trust), and Richard Arum and Josipa Roksa, *Academically Adrift: Limited Learning on College Campuses* (Chicago: University of Chicago, 2011).

157 most require at least one course: "Trends and Emerging Practices in General Education" set the figure at 62 percent. The survey had a 50 percent response rate, and 8 percent of the schools sampled were community colleges. My own check of 50 four-year schools by website – varied by Carnegie classification, selectivity, size, location, public/private – found that 75 percent have a diversity requirement and nearly 50 percent require at least two courses. The number of diversity courses showing up in other general education categories varies from 50 percent or more of the list to a few or none.

159 intellectual support from educational psychologists: See the works of Jerome Bruner, Charles Schwab, and others associated with the "structure of the disciplines" movement.

159 21ˢᵗ century Harvard college catalog: Harvard University's online catalog, 2005, section on the Core Curriculum.

8. LIBERAL LEARNING NEEDS A NEW PR CAMPAIGN

177 A 1989 Gallup survey: "A Survey of College Seniors: Knowledge of History and Literature," Gallup Organization, Princeton, NJ, 1989. Conducted for the National Endowment for the Humanities.

178 Another national survey of college seniors: "National College Senior Survey April 18-25, 1996," Roper Center for Public Opinion Research, University of Connecticut, Storrs, CT.

178 More unflattering data: "Losing America's Memory: Historical Illiteracy in the 21ˢᵗ Century," Center for Survey Research and Analysis (Roper),

University of Connecticut, Storrs, CT, 2000. Conducted for the American Council of Trustees and Alumni.

178 In 2006 and 2007 Roper surveyed: "Our Fading Heritage: Americans Fail a Basic Test on their History and Literacy," University of Connecticut Department of Public Policy (formerly Roper), Storrs, CT, 2007. Conducted for the Intercollegiate Studies Institute American Civic Literacy Program.

183 A good starting point: E.D. Hirsch, *Cultural Literacy: What Every American Needs to Know* (Boston: Houghton Mifflin, 1987).

186 Jacques Barzun has referred to: Jacques Barzun, "A Future for the Liberal Arts. If...," *Academic Questions* (Fall 1994).

187 Mortimer Adler has identified: Mortimer Adler, *The Great Ideas: A Syntopicon of the Western World* (Chicago: Encyclopedia Britannica, 1952).

INDEX

A

academic achievement, 60–64,
    114–115
academic mismatch
    affirmative-action admissions, ii,
      62, 64, 66, 76
    athletic admissions, 116, 122
academic support services, 114
acceleration, 136, 139, 141
acceptance rate, 30–31, 33, 43
accounting practices, 74, 109, 111
accreditation, 21, 143
accrediting agencies, 40, 141
ACT, 29, 38
acting white, 66
activity for its own sake, 102, 181
Adler, Mortimer, 187
administrators
    AP programs and, 127–128
    curriculum and, 174
    general education reform, 179
    high school, 129

    increase in, 7, 9
    salaries, 11
    sports and, 124
admissions committees, 47–48
admissions deans, 27, 30
admissions office
    alumni and, 87
    AP courses, 140, 143
    minority applicants, 61, 71
    NCAA and, 122
    qualification factors, 75
admissions preference, i, ii, 56, 67. *See
    also* affirmative action; big-
    time sports; legacies
admissions yield, 23
advanced degrees, 10, 136. *See also
    specific degree*
Advanced Placement (AP) program
    alternative solutions, 140–143
    college degree requirements,
      137–139
    college equivalence, 130–136

course content, 139–140

credits, 127–128, 137–138

growth of, 127–130

quality of, iii, 130

syllabus, 132–133, 139–140

teacher qualifications, 135–136

testing, 128–129, 132

affirmative action. *See* minority preference

affirmative action for the rich, 79

affordable alternatives, 18–22

African-American students

    admissions test scores, 61–62

    affirmative action class, 51–52

    civil rights movement, 80

    in law school, 62–64

    percentage plans, 72

    PH.D. programs, 64

African-American Studies, 154

alcohol, 117–119

alma mater, 70, 80, 82, 95, 111

alumni

    awards, 36

    boosters. *See* boosters

    cultivation of, 111

    legacies, 51–52, 79–97

alumni giving, ii, 8, 30, 31, 82, 87–88, 90–93

alumni network, 25, 45, 46–47, 49

amateur sports, ii, 102–105, 121–123

American Council of Trustees and Alumni, 41

American history, 80, 139, 146, 158, 160, 173

America's Best Colleges, 26

Andover, 128

Annapolis Group, 27

antebellum, 184

anti-intellectualism, 116–119, 123

anti-ranking approach, 34

AP. *See* Advanced Placement programs

appearance fees, 101

appropriation (state), 8

arena, 11, 102, 117, 121

Asian students, 52, 55, 72, 75, 77

Asian studies, 154

assistant coaches salaries, 11

athletes. *See also* big-time sports

    admission preferences, 51–52, 82

    amateur model, 121

    student-athletes, 103, 105, 113

athletic department, 101, 109, 110, 111

athletic scholarships, 105, 121

B

bachelor's degree

    community colleges and, 22

    degree requirements, 137

    future earnings, 5

    historical value of, 44, 47

    no-frills model, 20

    teaching requirement, 136

bake-sale principle, 108

Bakke v. University of California, 56

bar exam, 62–64

Barzun, Jacques, 186

basics (curriculum), 139, 147–148, 151

basketball. *See* big-time sports

beer and circus, 118, 123

begging the question, 159, 168

behavior modification, 188, 190

best black syndrome, 66

Bible courses, 192

big-time sports

    alternative model, 120–126

    amateur vs. professional, 100–108

    budget, 100, 106, 109–114

big-time teams, 100–101, 109, 114, 124

binge drinking, 117

black students. *See* African-American students

black studies, 58

Bohr, Niels, 169

boosters, 102, 110, 113, 120, 124

Brown vs. Board of Education, 189

budget

    sports, 100, 106, 109–114

    state funds decline, 7–8

    transparency in, 12–13, 109

C

California, 2, 56, 71

campus housing, 11–12, 58

Carnegie Mellon University, 19

CEOs, 45, 70

charitable deductions, 95

Chinese history, 160, 164

cinema

    on campus, 146

    history of, 160, 164

Civil Rights Act of 1866, 90

civil rights movement, 80, 152, 193

Civil War, 177, 181

CLA (Collegiate Learning Assessment), 35, 36, 37, 43

class bias, 37

class checkers, 114

class (culture), 153, 155, 156, 157

class rank, 33, 38

class size, 18, 32, 33, 39, 134

climbing wall, 12

club teams, 106

coaches, 113, 114, 124

coaches salaries, 11, 101

cognitive psychology, 188

College Board

    AP college-equivalence, 130, 133

    AP comparability studies, 142

    AP course content, 139–140

    AP demographics, 129

    AP program purview, 128

    school reviews, 27

college catalogs, iv, 40

college degree requirements, 137–139

College Navigator, 27

College Portrait, 27

College Search (website), 27

Collegiate Learning Assessment
(CLA), 35, 36, 37, 43

Common Data Set questionnaire, 39

community colleges

cost of, 2, 3

teacher requirements, 136

transfer students, 22–23

community relations, 111

comparability studies (AP program),
142

compelling societal interest, 56

compensatory justice, 53–60, 67, 72,
73

competition

among schools, 14, 73

for grades, 48

price, 6, 13, 21

for students, 80

computers, 7, 9, 166, 173

concerts, 12, 117

Congress

cost reporting requirements for
colleges, 15

legacy preference legislation, 96

tax exemption for sports, 107

congressional representatives, 45, 70

Constable, John, 185

construction, ii, 11, 109

consumers, 1–3, 13, 15, 21–22, 24, 44

content, 139–140

content knowledge, 158–165, 170–171

core curriculum, 174–175

core mission, 10, 13

counseling services, 9

critical theory, 150

critical thinking, 147, 159, 183

cultural literacy, 147, 152–158, 164,
183–186

curriculum

core curriculum, 174–175

defined, iii

designers, 160

distribution approach, 145–149

knowledge explosion, 165–170

modifications to, 170–176

politics in, 152–158, 171

prerequisite courses, 131–132

process and content distinction,
158–165, 170–171

ranking colleges and, 40–41

relativism in, 149–152, 164, 171

customized rankings, 42–43

D

debt, 3, 4, 13. *See also* financial aid;
grants; scholarships

Department of Education, U.S., 27

Derrida, Jacques, 150

development case, 94

development office, 8

disability services, 7

distribution approach to curriculum,
145–149

distributive justice, 58

diversity
    curriculum, 148, 152–158
    minorities, 52, 53–60
Division I
    academic mismatch, 122
    athletic programs, 109
    coaches, 124
    expenses, 112
    player commitments, 113, 116
    teams, 11, 110
Division I AA, 120
Division II, 120, 121, 124
Division III, 120, 122, 124
doctoral degree, 10, 64, 136
dominant institutional model, 17, 20
"due process of law," 168

E
early decision, 23
earnings potential, 46
electives, 172
elite colleges, 19, 64, 128, 179
endowments, 16–17
engineering schools, 31, 40
English composition, 41, 161
English departments, 162
enrollment, 6-7, 32, 39, 111
Epicurean, 185
ethnic studies, 154
European college students, 5
European higher education institutions, 5

Exeter, 128
exit testing, 37
expenditures
    from alumni giving, 92
    athletics, 111–112, 122
    mission creep and, 13
extracurricular programming, 23, 103, 152

F
faculty
    AP programs and, 128
    awards, 36
    growth of, 7, 9
    hiring, 13
    minorities as, 64
    quality of, 38–39
    salaries, 9, 33, 109
    specializations, 146, 172, 180
family, 81–82, 85–86, 187
federal government, 8, 14, 15, 24, 95, 96, 141
federal grants, 4, 8
federal mandates, 17
federal tax code, 95
financial aid. See also grants; scholarships
    admission preferences vs., 74
    college cost and, 4, 13–15
    college ranking and, 26
    private colleges, 95
financial need, 13–15

financing less expensive colleges, 21

1st Amendment, 94, 96, 159

Fish, Stanley, 150

food services, 109

football. *See* big-time sports

Forbes (magazine), 36

Fordham Institute, 135

foreign language, 41, 138, 143

for-profit colleges, 19

Fortune (magazine), 45, 70

Foucault, Michel, 150

foundational learning, 146–148

foundations, 8

Founders (American government), 89

14th Amendment, 89, 159, 168

freedom, 187, 191–194

freedom of association, 94

freshman retention rate, 31

freshman seminars, 179

freshmen

    enrollment, 23–24

    legacy preference, 80, 87, 93

    retention, 31, 38

    sports teams, 104

Freudianism, 150, 187-188,190

full-time faculty, 9, 31

fundraising, ii, 8, 30, 31, 82, 87–88,
    90–93

G

Gallup survey, 177-178

gender studies, 154

general education

    curriculum, 145–147, 171

    diversity in, 154

    process teaching, 158–165

    rating, 40–41

general intelligence, 186–187

Gettysburg Address, 178

GMAT. *See* Graduate Management
    Admission Test

government grants, 4, 8

"government of the people," 178

government subsidies, 6, 7–8

governors, 45, 70

grade inflation, 38

grade point average (GPA), 38

graduate assistants, 39

graduate education, ii, 10, 62

Graduate Management Admission
    Test (GMAT), 62

Graduate Record Examination
    (GRE), 61–62

graduate schools, 45, 47–49

graduate students, 33, 39

graduation rate, 31–32, 33, 38

grants. *See also* financial aid; scholar-
    ships

    federal, 4, 8

    foundations, 8

    institutions, 4

    merit, 4, 14

    Pell, 36

    Robin Hood principle, 3

state, 14

Great Ideas, 187

GRE, *See* Graduate Record Examina-
    tion

Grutter v. Bollinger, 56

guidance counselors, 87

H

Harvard University, 128, 131–132,
    159

Heisenberg, Werner, 169

hierarchy of knowledge, 172–173

high school diploma, 5, 137

high school GPA, 38

high school graduates, 6, 60, 61, 127

high schools. *See also* Advanced
        Placement (AP) programs
    guidance counselors, 30, 115
    percentage plans, 71–73

high school teachers, iii, 135–136

Hirsch, E.D., 183

Hispanic students
    admissions test scores, 61–62
    affirmative action group, 52
    civil rights movement, 80
    percentage plans, 72

Hispanic studies, 58, 154

historical literacy, 178

history
    American cinema, 160, 164
    Caribbean, 160, 164
    Chinese, 160, 164

curriculum, 41, 155, 163
    value of, 193–194

holistic admissions policies, 82–84

honors program, 137–138

humanistic psychology, 188

humanities, 138, 155, 168–169

hybrids (courses), 19

I

incentives (motivation), 4–5, 66

inclusion, 63, 129, 134

income, 2, 61, 74–75

inferiority, 65, 66, 72, 75, 189

inflation, 147, 179

information technology, 7

institutional grants, 4

institutional wealth, 33

international students, 29

internship, 46

interviewing skills, 46, 184

intramural teams, 106

introductory courses, 131, 143

investment, 5–6, 123

Ivy League, 28, 45

J

Jews, 80

job experience, 47

jobs, 113, 130, 195

job world, 2, 44, 194

justice, 57–59, 79–80, 157. *See also*
        compensatory justice

K

Kiplinger's (magazine), 36

Knowledge as relative, 148–152

knowledge explosion, 165–170

knowledge for its own sake, 182

L

Lady Macbeth, 184

Lake Wobegon, 130

laundry service, 12

Lawrenceville, 128

Law School Admission Test (LSAT),
      62

law schools, 62–63

law students, 62

leadership, 53–54, 70–71

learning

      foundational, 146–148

      liberal, 181–182

      online, 18–20

      traditional, 157–158

      vertical model, 138

      virtual, 18–20

lecture courses, 133–134

lecture method, 19

legacies, 51–52, 79–97

licensing standards, 63

literature, 41, 150, 155

loans, 14

lower division college, 136

low-income students, 73–75, 129

LSAT. *See* Law School Admission Test

M

Machiavellian, 184

magazines, cultural literacy and, 183

March Madness, 125

marine biology, 160, 174

master's degree, 10, 136–137, 147

MCAT. *See* Medical College Admission Test

mean (statistical measure), 185

median family income, 2

median (statistical measure), 185

Medical College Admission Test
      (MCAT), 62

Mendel, Gregor, 169

mental health counseling, 7

merit, 84–85

merit scholarships or grants, 4, 14

military recruiters, 96

mind, 188–189

minorities. *See also specific minority
      groups*

      advantaged, 55–56

      AP programs, 129

      leadership, 53–54, 70–71

minority preference, ii, 51–71, 76, 78,
      191.

      alternatives to, 71–76

minority studies, 58

MIT, 19–20

Monet, Claude, 159, 185

motorcycle helmets, 192, 196

multiculturalism, 152. *See* diversity

multicultural social programming, 7

multiplex student centers, 11

N

National Collegiate Athletic Association. *See* NCAA

National Survey of Student Engagement (NSSE), 35, 36

Native American students, 52

natural science, 41, 48, 138, 150

NCAA

    academic requirements, 114

    accounting monitoring, 122

    admission restrictions, 122

    commercial function, 122

    Division I expenses, 112

    Division I player commitments, 113, 116

    Division I teams, 11, 110

    division structure changes, 120

    employees, 125

    players earnings, 113

    purpose of, 102

    sports-related expenses, 109

need-based aid, 14

Nobility Clause (U.S. Constitution), 89

non-faculty professionals, 9

non-profit organizations, 16, 102, 107, 125

non-teaching personnel, 9

NSSE (National Survey of Student Engagement), 35, 36

O

online instruction, 18–20

online ranking systems, 42–43

operations and maintenance, 33

orientation, 143

outcome assessment, 35–37

P

party schools, 26, 118

peer assessment or review, 27, 30, 131

Pell grants, 36

pep rallies, 117

percentage plans, 71–73

Ph.D. programs, 64

Picasso, Pablo, 185

playing schedule, 11

playing season, 113

politics in curriculum, 152–158, 171

postmodernism, 85, 150, 159, 167

Powell (Justice), 56

practical knowledge, 183–186

practice schedules, 101

prestige factor, 20, 25, 43–49

price controls, 15–16

Princeton Review, 118

Princeton University, 128

process and content distinction, 158–165, 170–171, 172

professional schools, 10

professional team model, 120–126

professional vs. amateur sports, 100–108

profits, 17, 34, 102, 120

psychology, 155, 187–188

public funding, 95

publicity, 11, 112, 116, 124

public officials, v, 63, 126

public relations

    cultural literacy, 183–186

    educational quality surveys, 111, 177–179

    faculty, image of, 180

    general intelligence, 187–196

    liberal learning, image of, 181–182

    students expectations, 180–181

public service, ii, 10–11, 33

Q

quixotic, 159, 168

R

race, 52, 71–75, 83, 90, 194

racism, 146, 154, 189

rank in class, 33, 38

rap music, 192, 195

RateMyProfessors.com, 36

reading skills, 147, 159, 160–163

Reconstruction, 159, 177, 178

recruiting, 81, 86, 106, 124

relativism, 149–152, 164, 171

Rembrandt, 185

remedial students, 29, 129–130

remediation, 130, 161–162

research

    defined, 10

    faculty, 38–39

    federal funding, 95

    improvement in, iv

    spending, ii, 33

retention rate, 31–32, 33, 38

revenue-producing sports, 116

revolution, 187

Richter scale, 185

risk management, 7

Robin Hood principle, 3

room and board, 2, 12

Roper survey, 178-179

Rorty, Richard, 150

Row v. Wade, 147, 179

S

salaries

    administrators, 11

    coaches, 11

    faculty, 9, 33, 109

SAT scores

    affirmative action and, 71

    AP students and, 132

    college ranking and, 29, 31, 33, 38, 43

    legacy students and, 83

    minority groups and, 60–62

scholarships. *See also* financial aid; grants

    athletic, 105, 121

    merit, 4, 14

scientific knowledge, 169–170

scientific method, 164

segregated schools, 72, 77, 189

selective colleges, 55, 60–61, 68–69,
        71–72, 122, 128

Senators, U.S., 45, 70, 147

seniors
    college, 177–178, 179
    high school, 35–36, 128–129, 141

sequential courses, 131

sexual harassment policies, 152

Shakespeare, William, 155, 181, 184

The Shape of the River (book), 70

signage, 101, 121

skills, 68, 100, 121–122, 147, 175. *See
        also specific skills*

skyboxes, 102

smorgasbord model, 172. *See also*
        curriculum

social inequality, 156–157

social justice, 16, 157

social science, 138, 150, 155

social utility, 82, 88, 93

specialized courses, iii, 40, 138, 163, 171

spending per student, 33

sponsored programs, 8

stadiums, 11, 101, 102, 117

standard deviation, 185

Stanford University, 19

state funding, 6, 7–8

stereotype threat, 66

strict scrutiny, 56

student-athletes, 103, 105, 113

student/faculty ratio, 32

student services, 33

superego, 184, 187–188

support services, 7, 9, 33, 114

Supreme Court (U.S.), 56, 88–90, 96

survey courses, 41, 147

surveys of educational quality,
        177–179

Swarthmore, 128

swimming, 110, 125

T

tax
    income, 121
    tuition as, 3

tax-exemption, 106–108

teaching assistants, 136

teaching load, 10

teaching process, 158–165, 170–171,
        172

team travel, 106

television and sports, 101, 104

test optional policy, 29, 38

Texas, 71

ticket sales, 121

Title IX, 7

track and field, 125

traditional knowledge, 153–154, 158

training rooms, 12

training schedules, 115

transcripts, 143, 146

transfers, 20, 23–24, 113

travel

    calculations, 178

    cost, 106

    sports teams, 11, 116

travel schedules, 116

trustees, v, 41, 174

tuition

    control of, 17–18

    cost of, 2

    purpose of, ii

tuition wavers, 101

tutoring, 12, 114

twentieth century, iv, 43–44, 80, 90, 149, 152, 165, 169

U

unconscious mind, 188–189

undergraduate instruction, 10–13, 24

universalism, 151

University and College Accountability Network, 27

university press, vi

U.S. Constitution, 139, 177

    freedoms granted in, 193

    1st Amendment, 94, 96, 159

    5th Amendment, 159

    14th Amendment, 89, 159

U.S. House of Representatives, 15, 45, 70, 96, 107

U.S. News and World Report (magazine), 26–35

utilitarianism, 94, 181-182

V

varsity athletes, 110, 121, 123

varsity sports, 104, 122

vertical model of learning, 138, 139

victimhood, 65–66, 75

violence, 157

virtual learning, 18–20

W

wars, 139, 164, 187, 193

Washington (city), 15, 95

Washington Monthly (magazine), 36

weighting factors (college ranking), 33–34, 42

Western culture, 153–158

Western tradition, 180, 187

WhatWillTheyLearn.com, 41

white guilt, 54

white man's burden, 77

The Wizard of Oz, 185

women's studies, 154

wrestling, 110

writing across the curriculum, 162

writing-intensive, 161–162

writing skills, 159–162

Y

Yale University, 19

year-round commitment, 11, 113

www.ingramcontent.com/pod-product-compliance
Lightning Source LLC
Chambersburg PA
CBHW062203080426

42734CB00010B/1773